When GOD says NO

BY **WILLIAM P. BARKER**

EVERYONE IN THE BIBLE
THEY STOOD BOLDLY
SAINTS AND SWINGERS
WOMEN AND THE LIBERATOR
WHEN GOD SAYS NO

When GOD says NO

William P. Barker

FLEMING H. REVELL COMPANY
OLD TAPPAN, NEW JERSEY

Unless otherwise identified, Scripture references in this volume are from the Revised Standard Version of the Bible, copyrighted 1946 and 1962.

Scripture references identified KJV are from the King James Version of the Bible.

Scripture references identified NEB are from the New English Bible. © The Delegates of the Oxford University Press and the Syndics of the Cambridge University Press 1961 and 1970. Reprinted by permission.

Library of Congress Cataloging in Publication Data

Barker, William Pierson.
  When God says no.

  1. Bible—Biography. 2. Providence and government
of God. I. Title.
BS571.B344   220.9'2 [B]   73–18148
ISBN 0–8007–0643–9

TO
all in the church family
at First Presbyterian Church of Allentown

Acknowledgments

Several persons deserve special verbal bouquets for their assistance in preparing this book. Miss Martha Sammis typed and proofread the manuscript. Mrs. Viola Allerton and Mrs. Pat Fainor also proofread. Richard K. White, M.D. provided many helpful insights. John K. Stoner, Harry L. Holfelder, and Douglas G. McKenzie gave numerous excellent suggestions. Fred M. Rogers, as always, offered countless meaningful ideas. G. D. McRae, Raymond Hill, and the Luxor Ministerial Association rendered their usual creative support. Finally, Jean, Ellen, Jock, and Sandy surrounded me with their constant love and encouragement!

Contents

Introduction

Sometimes, we don't get our wishes. God apparently turns us down.

Why? Is God deaf? Doesn't He care?

The following fourteen "case studies" from the Bible show that God sometimes refuses our requests because He *does* care and because He has other plans.

There are no cardboard characters in the Bible. Every personality in Scripture faced the same ambitions and anxieties as anyone alive today. Some wanted to escape pressures. Others wanted to build monuments so that they would be remembered. Some grew so sour and depressed that they wanted to quit everything—even life itself. All faced problems, disappointment, illness, and death.

Each of the following biblical characters represents a different situation. Each pleaded that God go along with his plans. Each learned to accept God's *no*—and to be grateful for it.

These studies are intended to help us, God's people today, to reflect on His involvement in our lives now, especially when He apparently refuses to accede to all our requests. Most of all, these studies are meant to show that although God sometimes must give us a negative reply, through Jesus Christ by the Holy Spirit today He continually offers positive opportunities!

The prayer of an unknown Confederate soldier hints at what this means:

I asked God for strength, that I might achieve,
I was made weak, that I might learn humbly to obey.
I asked for health, that I might do greater things,
I was given infirmity, that I might do better things.
I asked for riches, that I might be happy,
I was given poverty that I might be wise.
I asked for power, that I might have the praise of men,
I was given weakness, that I might feel the need of God.
I asked for all things, that I might enjoy life,
I was given life, that I might enjoy all things.
I got nothing that I asked for—but everything I had hoped
  for,
Almost despite myself, my unspoken prayers were answered.
I am among all men, most richly blest.

WILLIAM P. BARKER

When GOD says NO

1

Abraham,
who hoped everything would stay put

Of all the cities in the Old Testament world, you and I would have been most at home in Abraham's birthplace or boyhood city. Ur and Haran, Abraham's home cities, had nearly every fascinating facet of modern metropolitan life, from poetry forums to pollution, from two-story homes to traffic problems!

Abraham was born in Ur, the capital of a great commercial empire which controlled all of Mesopotamia and extended to Anatolia. Abraham felt immensely safe and secure, for Ur symbolized a civilization which challenged nature with a boldness and success which was never matched until the Americans lived four thousand years later!

Abraham grew up with a sense of pride in being a man of Ur. Ur, he knew, was the cradle of a culture of "firsts." Here was the society where nameless inventive geniuses first had wheeled vehicles rolling on a grid of city streets (and also produced the world's first traffic jams). Here stood the first libraries and schools. Here were written the world's first codified rational laws to govern human behavior. Here, not Egypt or Babylon or Greece, democracy was invented, and here the concept of empire was born. Here also was the birthplace of the column, the arch, vault, and dome in architecture.

No one, Abraham reflected, could threaten Ur or its great empire. Its military prowess was unmatched. It had invented the phalanx (the B–52 of its time), the superweapon which devastated opposition and made Ur undisputed master of Mesopotamia.

When Abraham walked through Ur, he saw splendor every-where. Tall, attractive women passed, wearing cosmetics and beautifully crafted jewelry. Ur, Abraham understood, was also the center for the arts. Ur's wealth attracted the best artisans. Abraham admired the women's exquisite headpieces, fashioned into delicate, beaten-gold leaves, and the meticulously dainty necklaces and bracelets. Abraham knew the spacious homes in Ur, where servants served guests in silver goblets shaped by artists with superb skills and taste.

Abraham enjoyed the intellectual excitement which per-meated Ur. Ur's libraries and schools made the city a center for learning and research. Scholars had developed tables in math-ematics and formulas for extracting square and cube roots. De-signers had perfected precision in measurements almost une-qualed until our day. Hydraulic engineers had designed devices to carry water to heights eighty feet above ground level. Abraham inherited the benefits and enjoyed the comforts of a sophisticated technology.

Abraham's home city, with gorgeous gardens and ample, open spaces, seemed almost like a vast park. Courtyards, arches, and gates, expertly designed and faultlessly constructed, adorned the lovely landscape. The royal palace, an opulently magnificent edifice, occupied one section of the city.

Abraham and everyone in Ur, however, took greatest civic pride in the ziggurat. The ziggurat, a magnificent temple to the moon-god, Nanna, dominated the city. It was a skyscraper shrine looming so high over the city that Abraham noticed it every time he went outside his house.

The ziggurat was approached through a great towered gate. It stood in a vast courtyard in which niches had been built for all the known deities who presumably met in assembly with Nanna, the moon-god. Across the entrance court rose an enor-mous set of stairs leading to an even larger court on a great terrace, standing above all the buildings in the city. This court and terrace were ringed by a marvelously designed set of rooms for the ceremonials and priests' residences. In the center of this huge court ascended the ziggurat itself—a kind of pyramid in three massive stages or steps.

The walls of this gigantic structure were seventy-seven feet thick at the base, which may give some idea of the size of the ziggurat. The ziggurat was so expertly engineered and constructed that it stood 1,750 years without any repairs or alterations!

On each of the three steps or stages of this towering pyramid were terraced, beautifully landscaped courtyards, with stairways sweeping upward to the next level. High above Ur on the topmost layer of the three-stage sacred tower reposed the shrine of Nanna. Within the walls of every level was built a honeycomb of passages, storage areas, living quarters, and worship centers. In spite of its sheer bulk, the ziggurat was beautifully designed with sloping walls to give the appearance of soaring height.

Abraham and everyone in Ur felt a sense of satisfaction from residing in the metropolis with the ziggurat, with learning, with culture, and wealth.

Although Abraham moved from Ur to Haran as a young man, he did not feel as if he had left the center of the universe. First of all, he knew that Haran meant a continuation of the same life-style as Ur's. Haran perpetuated everything that Ur stood for. Second, Abraham knew that Haran also had class and excitement. Although not the great capital, Haran boasted a sophistication of its own. Abraham quickly adjusted to Haran, his adopted city.

Haran, in Sumerian, means caravan town. In Abraham's time, Haran stood as the transportation and trade capital, the major center for the caravans which crisscrossed the ancient world. These caravans, sometimes with three thousand donkeys in one train, were the transport system in the ancient world. Haran, occupying the northern end of the richest and busiest trade route, and sitting astride the matrix of a network of subsidiary roads, was to Ur what Chicago is to the United States.

Abraham quickly found himself caught up with the warmth and energy which pulsated through Haran. He liked the enthusiasm of its people. He found that he could make a comfortable living in Haran. Infected with a zest for Haran, Abraham prepared to settle down.

Ur and Haran were part of a disciplined, structured society which seems peculiarly similar to our own. It was prosperous and orderly, strong and enduring. At times, it even seems oddly appealing. Ombudsmen cut through bureaucratic red tape. Slaves could buy their freedom, fight court cases, get married. Children argued with their teachers. Like us, Ur and Haran admired wealth, possessions, and good food, but quoted proverbs in praise of the simple life. Again like us, Ur and Haran showed themselves crassly materialistic, yet professed deep spiritual roots.

Abraham, in fact, found himself surrounded with plenty of religion in both Ur and Haran. Nanna's impressive sanctuary in Ur, the ziggurat, stood as a perpetual reminder of religion's place in society. Haran boasted of its own great shrine and cult to the moon-god, who, in Haran, went locally by the name *Sin*. Haran, by Abraham's time, was renowned as the headquarters for the worship of the moon-god throughout the world.

Life in Haran brought comfort and contentment to Abraham. Most of all, however, Abraham appreciated his family. Ties of kinship meant much in the ancient Middle East. Relatives provided protection to the individual. Without the prestige and support of a large, strong family, a lone man stood in constant danger.

Abraham felt grateful that his father, Terah, and his brothers, Nahor and Haran, and their offspring lived near him in Haran. The family was close-knit. Abraham enjoyed the frequent reunions, the civic holidays, and family celebrations, when the entire clan gathered for dinner. The warm, supportive circle of relatives reinforced Abraham's sense of personal identity and worth. It helped Abraham to have old Terah or his brothers to talk over plans and problems. Abraham appreciated all that his family meant to him and did for him. He looked forward to a long, happy, useful lifetime in Haran, surrounded by a large neighborhood of children, grandchildren, cousins, nephews, nieces, and other kinfolk. In time, Abraham mused, he would be admired as one of the city's leading citizens. He anticipated the time when he would be venerated in Haran and Ur as the patriarch of a sizable and influential clan.

Abraham married a beautiful girl named Sarah. He expected his version of the Haran dream to come true. The only factor which ruffled Abraham's happy life in Haran was the fact that he and Sarah had no baby. Although Abraham felt disappointed that he had not immediately fathered an heir, he nonetheless smiled contentedly. Life with Sarah and his big family in Haran was good. What more could a man want? Abraham anticipated living out his years in Haran. He was secure. He was comfortable.

Leave Haran? Never! Turn his back on his sheltered, pleasant life? Tear himself away from his family? What stupidity!

The first time Abraham became aware of the thought—it came more like an abrupt command to him than an idle thought—of leaving Haran's beloved faces and luxuries, he laughed to himself. He tried to dismiss the notion.

He found himself confronted again with instructions to go out from Haran. Why, Abraham puzzled to himself, why did he seem to be badgered by this absurd idea? It began to seem as if someone were repeatedly planting this notion in his thinking. Who?

Another—the Other—persisted in addressing Abraham.

Abraham could not understand himself for taking the Other seriously. After all, Abraham insisted, he could not even see or hear, touch or smell the One who insisted on intruding on his thinking with such unreasonable demands.

Abraham argued with himself, "This impossible order that I keep receiving . . . if it has to do with religion, why isn't the moon-god involved in it? After all, as everyone knows in Haran, all genuine light and wisdom comes from Sin, the lunar deity." The moon-god, he discovered, issued no troubling directions.

Abraham, however, kept receiving a disturbing signal, not from the moon-god enshrined in Haran, but from the Eternal One, hidden yet present. "Go," Abraham understood the Disturber to be instructing him. "Go from your country and your kindred and your father's house to the land that I will show you" (Genesis 12:1).

Abraham did not want to go. He intended to stay in Haran.

Rip loose from everyone and everything which supported

him and kept him going? Break with his family? Leave his friends? Walk away from Haran's lights and parties? Forget his investments and retirement plan? What kind of a god would ever make such outrageous demands? Abraham mused that it would be better to stick with the moon-god of Haran.

The Voice could not be stilled. The orders—never requests, Abraham noticed, but always commands—repeatedly pounded on Abraham's consciousness.

Abraham began to find himself in dialogue with the Unseen One.

Wait a minute, Lord. You want me to leave all this —to go out to some unknown place? You insist that I face the uncertainty of the desert? with no more safety than a tent?

Look, Lord. Sarah and I are comfortable here. I'm just getting on my feet in my business. The place is fixed up the way we like it. We're in a position to do a few things now. All our people live here—my father and my brothers and all the family. Our get-togethers and the holidays mean a lot. We want to stay put. We're settled and happy here. Leave us alone!

Besides, Lord, I must think of my security. How do I know things will work out if I leave Haran? What kind of proofs can You give me that I'll be satisfied? For that matter, how do I know that this whole wild scheme is not a dream or fantasy?

If You are so interested in me, Lord, and if You really want to do something, how about boosting my business? If You insist on hanging around me, make me feel more secure. Let me have some peace of mind. Help me get ahead!

The Other, in effect, replied, *No, Abraham, I have not come for idle chitchat. I will not be used. I refuse to be exploited in order to promote business or serenity or anything. I—not you —give the orders.*

My orders, Abraham, as I have been trying to make clear to

*you, are that you are to trust Me and obey Me. However, I offer
you no advantages, no secret deals for obeying Me. You are to
trust Me because I am God, and you are to obey because I have
chosen you.*

Abraham heard no souped-up sales talks from God. Nor did
Abraham receive travel folders and full-color brochures on the
joys of being a homeless nomad out West. No Chamber of Com-
merce speeches on the blandishments of Canaan. No return-
trip ticket back to Haran in case things didn't work out. No
money-back guarantee that the venture into the unknown
would be successful. Abraham received only the repeated summons, *Get packed and move out! Trust and obey Me!*

Abraham remonstrated, "But what practical sense . . . ?"

God answered, *No, Abraham, there is no so-called practical
sense to what I'm asking you—at least from your standpoint.
Ever. My demands are emotionally difficult. My orders are
financially absurd. You will lose every shred of security. You
will pull up all your roots.*

"Yes, but . . ." Abraham insisted, "where is it all heading?
What's the point? What are You doing to me? I don't like the
unknown. I prefer everything tidy and safe. Please, let me stay
here in Haran where I am happy!"

Abraham's request was turned down. Sometimes God says *no!*

Instead of being allowed to remain in dazzling, affluent Haran and Ur, with joyous family gatherings and a paid-up mort-
gage, Abraham was ordered to move out.

Why was the Lord ordering him to venture into the unknown? The reason given for leaving Haran: God promised a
permanent home for his hundreds of descendants!

But there was more, God indicated. Not only would
Abraham's many descendants have a permanent home, but
they would be God's blessing poured out on all mankind. A
blessing, Abraham understood, was an outpouring of God's life
and health-giving power. God's purpose, He made clear to
Abraham, was that Abraham's family be passerson of God's
enlivening strength to all the families on earth!

Was all this a put-on? Was God pulling a mean joke? Abraham
smiled bitterly. Hundreds of descendants? This stung. Abraham

did not even have *one* descendant. To his intense disappointment, Sarah had not been able to have any children. God's blithe assurance that Abraham's progeny would populate a Promised Land bordered on bad taste, Abraham thought.

Not only did Abraham have no children, but this so-called Promised Land was hundreds of miles away and owned by powerful, hostile tribes. Venture across wild country to settle some real estate among uncultured foreigners?

When Abraham tried to explain all of this to his urbane friends at the club, he realized more deeply what folly he was up to. They could not understand why he would leave the civilized comforts and pleasant amenities of Haran and Ur to follow such a wispy idea.

Telling his family proved to be even more difficult. No matter how Abraham tried to explain it, he seemed to imply that he no longer wanted to be with his relatives. He could tell that they were hurt. Although he reassured them that he loved them, he sensed that they felt rebuffed.

The pain of approaching separation grew more intense. Sometimes Abraham felt like shrieking, "Let me alone, Lord! I do not want to go. Let me stay here."

God's answer to Abraham's plea remained a firm *no.* However, God repeated that He was turning down Abraham's request to remain in Haran because of a purpose and a promise. "And I will make of you a great nation, and I will bless you, and make your name great, so that you will be a blessing . . . and by you all the families of the earth will bless themselves" (Genesis 12:2, 3).

Abraham obeyed. He left Haran. He embarked for the unknown; ". . . he went out, not knowing where he was to go" (Hebrews 11:8). He turned his back for good on everything which sheltered and protected him. He could not see his destination. He blinked back the tears, aware that he would never see kin or friends. Taking the risk of faith, Abraham walked out of Haran with little more than a sense of God's purpose and God's promise. As he trudged along the road that first day, he remembered the farewell parties, the final dinner with all the family, the weeping, and the last embraces. Abraham reflected that a purpose and a promise from God were, after all, fragile reasons to give up the good life in Ur and Haran.

Later, when his descendants described him, they spoke of Abraham as "a wandering Aramean" (Deuteronomy 26:5), which in Hebrew also means straying or perishing. In their eyes, Abraham had been like a helpless, stray lamb, exposed to deadly perils. Cut off from family and home, living as a wanderer meant Abraham had to exist completely without the shelter and support of those closest and dearest, and therefore in constant mortal danger.

Years and years later, Abraham was still wandering. He was also still reflecting on God's purpose for him, and pondering God's promise to him. Abraham was still living in a tent. A tent, he reminded himself, was far from being the solid, comfortable residences he had known in Ur and Haran. Abraham knew from experience what flimsy, impermanent shelter a tent provides. That tent, flapping in every wind, put up and taken down thousands of times since leaving Haran, symbolized being a transient. Abraham realized each day that he was homeless.

True, Abraham remembered, after years of waiting, God had come through—finally—with a son for Abraham and Sarah. After the son, Isaac, had been given to them in their old age, it appeared that God was going back on His purpose and His promise because it had looked as if God meant to take the boy. Abraham recalled the doubts which he harbored toward God, the agony which he had felt over the possible loss of his little boy, the relief he experienced when young Isaac was spared to grow up.

Finally, Sarah, Abraham's wife, died. He was alone. He faced the bleak emptiness of old age. The Carborundum of time had worn down Abraham's powers, and Abraham realized that he was frail and aged. He knew that he, too, would soon die.

This weary, feeble, old man was still a rootless alien. Abraham still wandered, still slept in a tent, still shuffled toward an uncertain destination.

The Promised Land? Not for Abraham. The only piece of ground he owned was a small cemetery lot in which Sarah was buried. Even this tiny piece of real estate was situated in an unfriendly area.

The promised descendants? Abraham sighed. His son was not

married and there were no grandchildren for him to see.

Abraham wondered if the only permanency in his long years of wandering was a forgotten grave far from home. What did he have to cling to?

A purpose. And a promise. Abraham could lie down and let death do its worst because God's purpose and God's promise still stood! Abraham was optimistic that the Lord would not go back on His word. Abraham knew that he had already seen enough evidence that God's refusal to let him stay in Haran was right. Abraham sat contently in his final days because he had confidence in God's purpose.

Like Abraham, we will often find that God's purpose for us seems obscured by setbacks, heartaches, frustrations, tensions, and separations. We modern Abrahams, however, are sustained by not simply a promise, but by the Promise of God which was fleshed out in Jesus.

Jesus Christ embodies the Promise of God for us. Through the cues of the Holy Spirit to us each day, we latter-day Abrahams are reminded that Jesus Christ's death and Resurrection are God's undying Promise that His love and faithfulness follow us, all the days of our wandering! Because of His Promise, we aliens in a strange land, far from home, may continue the pilgrimage with confidence and joy!

2

Moses,
who longed to see his dreams completed

Moses had no intention in getting involved. He had already learned his lesson on what getting involved meant. Years earlier, as a fiery-tempered young man, certain that he was unobserved, he had struck and killed an Egyptian who had been beating a Hebrew. The following day, thinking that no one knew about the Egyptian, Moses had tried to break up an argument between two Hebrews. The two Hebrews turned on Moses. One snarled, "Who made you a prince and a judge over us? Do you mean to kill me as you killed the Egyptian?" (Exodus 2:14).

Moses realized that he was not only rejected by his own people, the Hebrews, but would be quickly picked up for murder by the Egyptian police. He fled the country. He resolved never again to get mixed up in either Hebrew or Egyptian affairs. No one appreciated his efforts, he decided, and he would just as soon look after good old Number One—Moses.

He had scurried out of the reaches of Egyptian justice to Midian, married, settled down, and enjoyed the easygoing life of a desert rancher. He looked after his spread in Midian and told himself that the world would be a better place if everyone just minded his own business.

He had never thought of himself as a religious man. Consequently, he was disturbed one day when he was confronted by a strange sight. Before him, a desert shrub stood wreathed in flames yet did not burn up. Moses grasped at once that the burning bush symbolized the Eternal who gives yet is none the poorer, the Mighty Other who is the Source of all power yet is never exhausted, the Creator who works yet never wearies, the Compassionate One who cares, whose goodness never needs replenishing. Furthermore, this searing experience, Moses understood, reintroduced him to the One whom his mother had spoken about even when Moses was a spoiled, Egyptianized princeling. Moses trembled. He sensed that he could never evade the Deity who meant to claim him just as He had branded Moses' ancestors: "I am the God of your father, the God of Abraham, the God of Isaac, and the God of Jacob" (Exodus 3:6).

God, Moses quickly discovered, does not give private revelations as party favors to be taken home and treasured quietly in leisure moments. Instead, Moses found himself jolted by the high-voltage announcement that God heard the groans and cries of the Hebrews suffering in Egypt.

God's next news to Moses exploded with terrifying directness: "I will send you to Pharaoh that you may bring forth my people, the sons of Israel, out of Egypt" (Exodus 3:10).

Moses objected violently. Go back to Egypt and get mixed up in Egyptian politics and Hebrew labor? Never. Moses did not want trouble.

Up until this point, the burning bush scene had been a meaningful spiritual experience for Moses. He could go along with *feeling* religious. Moses could even engage in some God talk. But suddenly it appeared that God was getting entangled in government and business with His commands and concerns about the oppressive Pharaoh and those hurting Hebrews. Moses had already had problems enough with Egyptian authorities and Hebrew workers. He had vowed that he would not get involved again.

God insisted.

Moses squirmed angrily. He protested, "Who am I that I should go to Pharaoh, and bring the sons of Israel out of Egypt?" (Exodus 3:11), whimpering that he was a nobody, an insignificant rancher from the sticks.

Besides, Moses continued, if he ever would go to Egypt, how could he tell the shiftless Hebrews about the God they had neither heard about nor cared about? "If I come to the people of Israel and say to them, 'The God of your fathers has sent me to you,' and they ask me, 'What is his name?' what shall I say to them?" (Exodus 3:13).

Moses pointed out to God that he would be ignored in the Hebrew slave camps and laughed out of the Egyptian palace. No one would take him seriously. "They will not believe me or listen to my voice, for they will say, 'The Lord did not appear to you' " (Exodus 4:1). Moses did not relish being the subject of jokes.

Furthermore, Moses pleaded that he was not a compelling speaker. "I am not eloquent . . . I am slow of speech and of tongue" (Exodus 4:10). Moses advised the Lord to find someone else.

Moses threw all the excuses in the book at the Lord. God batted them down, one by one.

Moses, the man who tried to beg off from serving God, reluctantly responded. He allowed himself to be convinced by God that he had to involve himself with his Hebrew cousins who were herded out of squalid labor compounds each dawn into the enervating heat to work until dusk in the royal brickyards of Pharaoh Rameses II.

Moses quickly discovered that Rameses II had no intention of recognizing Moses' claims. The pompous, arrogant Pharaoh snickered when Moses announced that the Lord wanted His people to be freed. The Hebrews, the Pharaoh haughtily announced, were *his* people, not the Lord's. Moreover, sneered the vain Rameses II, who had taken all the titles of all gods, and liked to be referred to as the "Gracious Lord" and the "Giver of Life," "Who is the Lord, that I should heed his voice and let Israel go? I do not know the Lord, and moreover I will not let Israel go" (Exodus 5:2).

The Pharaoh angrily ordered the Hebrews back to work. Figuring that the Israelites had too much idle time on their hands and would be more docile if they were kept busier, Rameses II informed them that their output of bricks would stay the same but from then on they would have to secure the straw on their own.

Moses suddenly found himself resented by the very people he

had come to save. He realized that he had only made matters worse for the Hebrews. Already working to the point of collapsing and dying in the seven-days-a-week, never-ending production line, they had, in effect, had their quota of bricks increased. Moses berated himself for causing their burdens to grow heavier.

Bitterly, Moses accused the Lord. "Lord, why hast thou done evil to this people? Why didst thou ever send me? For since I came to Pharaoh to speak in thy name, he has done evil to this people, and thou hast not delivered thy people at all" (Exodus 5:22,23).

A terrible series of natural disasters followed. The water level of the Nile fell, and foul, stagnant pools collected along the muddy banks. Frogs appeared everywhere. The sun and heat killed the frogs, however, and millions of dead frogs littered the land. Gnats and flies, attracted by the decaying frogs, multiplied and swarmed throughout every village. Infection and disease began to break out. A devastatingly heavy hailstorm suddenly descended on the Nile valley, destroying livestock and grain crops. The winds also blew in hordes of locusts, which devoured everything green and growing throughout the land. Terrifying sandstorms followed, darkening the skies for days. Capping these ghastly catastrophes, a deadly epidemic swept through all Egyptian families, carrying off the youngest and weakest.

Taking advantage of the disorganized state of affairs in the Pharaoh's palace, Moses mobilized the Hebrews in the slave camps to depart. He ordered them to prepare to move out immediately, not even to wait for the next day's bread to rise. To delay meant dying like the Egyptians, Moses harshly warned. God, he promised, would enable them to pass over from death to life, from captivity to freedom!

Moses hurried the horde of frightened, undisciplined refugees eastward. They were forced to stop by the wide marshes of the Red Sea which stretched before them. Suddenly, Moses heard someone scream, "The Egyptians are coming!" Looking back, Moses saw the dust cloud above the armored divisions, Pharaoh's crack troops, on their way to slay and capture the escapees.

Panic seized the Hebrews. Hysterically, they shrieked at Moses, "Is it because there are no graves in Egypt that you have taken us away to die in the wilderness? What have you done to us, in bringing us out of Egypt? Is not this what we said to you in Egypt, 'Let us alone and let us serve the Egyptians'? For it would have been better for us to serve the Egyptians than to die in the wilderness" (Exodus 14:11,12).

To everyone, the situation appeared hopeless. Trapped between the water and the oncoming Egyptian chariots, the wailing Hebrews told each other that because of that meddler, Moses, they would all be dead by morning.

Moses silently bore the stinging accusations. He longed only to see the ordeal over, to get his charges into the Promised Land, and to be done with them.

During the night, a God-sent wind blew back the waters from the marshes, and Moses herded the remnants from the slave stockades across to safety. By the time the Egyptians with their heavy equipment started through the marshes in pursuit, the wind abruptly shifted. The waters oozed back, miring the chariots and eventually drowning the Pharaoh's army. God had miraculously delivered the oppressed wretches from the labor gangs of Rameses II!

Moses' mission, however, was not accomplished. Although he had led them out of Egypt, he still had not delivered them to Canaan. Moses became increasingly obsessed with getting into the Promised Land and being released from his assignment. He did not know it at the time, but it would take them forty years and at the end he would not be allowed to live to enter Canaan.

Refugees from forced-labor battalions are poor material to forge a nation of conquerors, Moses quickly learned. Cowed and supine from years of defeat, Moses' Hebrews proved to be easily demoralized. Moses was puzzled as to why God decided to select this motley crew of sniveling complainers to be His people. Why hadn't He chosen a hardy band of disciplined adventurers, some self-reliant, pioneer types, instead of these whipped puppies?

Moses had hardly scoutmastered them across the marshes after God's intervention when they began to grouse about the lack of water. Moses, hardened by years of desert living, grew impatient at their criticisms. What did they expect, Moses thought to himself, a stroll through an oasis? After all, they were fleeing for their lives and were intending to settle in Canaan. Moses, with the Lord's guidance, patiently secured water.

Moses had hardly met the first water crisis when the sullen Israelites began to carp about the food. "Would that we had died by the hand of the Lord in the land of Egypt, when we sat by the fleshpots and ate bread to the full; for you have brought us out into this wilderness to kill this whole assembly with hunger" (Exodus 16:3), they yammered, forgetting the hardships in the brickyards.

Although Moses met each situation and, with the Lord's help, provided for the Israelites, the crescendo of complaints rose. Tempers grew shorter. Accusations grew sharper. A second time, the Hebrews—spoiled by years of living with ample water supply in Egypt—accused Moses, "Why did you bring us up out of Egypt, to kill us and our children and our cattle with thirst?" (Exodus 17:3). Ugly rumors reached Moses that some were even discussing plans to stone him. Wearily, Moses arranged again for the entire group to find water in time to survive.

The journey stretched out into months, then years. Instead of making directly for Canaan, the Promised Land, they were forced to make wide detours to the south, avoiding clashes with inhospitable sheiks. Even so, Moses and the Israelites brushed with a band of toughs headed by a desert chief named Amalek. Moses discovered a bold, young fighter in his ranks named Joshua, who rallied enough Hebrew men to beat off the attacking Amalekites. Although he had a promising warrior and strategist in Joshua, Moses knew that the Israelites, still flabby and disorganized, were far from ready to take on the rugged, seasoned defenders of Canaanite cities.

Moses sighed as he thought of what a relief it would be to cross into Canaan at last and take possession of the area promised by God. The dream of entering the Promised Land sustained Moses after exhausting days of conflict and decisions. Moses' indomitable will seemed to be the only driving force within the entire group. Finally, to take some of the leadership load from his shoulders, Moses appointed some subleaders to help handle the ceaseless complaints.

Obviously, however, the entire body of Israelites would eventually have to acquire a sense of direction. Long months of camping together had not welded them into anything more than a rabble of escapees. In spite of God's mighty act of deliverance at the Red Sea, few of the number had any inkling of God's rule or God's intentions.

Moses gathered the entire encampment. God, Moses announced, had miraculously brought them safely out of Egypt. In return, He expected them to obey Him as a special people. In fact, according to Moses, God offered to make a solemn pact or covenant with the Israelites.

To Moses' relief, everyone agreed. The Israelites promised to be God's own, "a kingdom of priests and a holy nation" (Exodus 19:6). God and Moses' Hebrews contracted to be faithful to each other.

Moses next announced that God would disclose His charter for His people. Taking his trusted subleaders with him, Moses clambered up through the heavy clouds and disappeared from sight. The others, waiting below in the eerie valley, coaxed Moses' brother Aaron to help them to devise a homemade religious celebration. Together, they fashioned a metal bull, a popular and ubiquitous symbol of a Canaanite fertility cult, and began a wild orgy. When Moses returned to the camp with the Ten Commandments and came upon the debauchery, he was incensed.

It galled Moses to discover that his Israelites could slip so easily into such depraved paganism. Even his brother Aaron, the priest of the Israelites, weakly absolved himself of responsibility. Moses, furious at the apostasy, shouted, "Who is on the Lord's side? Come to me" (Exodus 32:26). A brief but bloody skirmish erupted between those who chose to return to Moses and those who rejected him to continue their erotic revelry.

Moses almost wept. Then he prayed. In his prayer, Moses interceded for his Israelites. He pleaded with the Lord to forgive them, adding ". . . and if not, blot me, I pray thee, out of thy book which thou hast written" (Exodus 32:32). In the depths of his despair, Moses nonetheless identified with his people so much that he was willing to be the scapegoat for their irresponsibility.

To his astonishment, however, Moses heard the Lord's orders to get moving again toward the Promised Land. Moses hoped that the journey would soon end and he would be able to sit down in the Promised Land without leadership burdens.

Moses, his nerves frazzled from too many years of coping with crises, pleaded with the Lord, "I am not able to carry all this people alone, the burden is too heavy for me. If thou wilt deal thus with me, kill me at once . . . that I may not see my wretchedness" (Numbers 11:14,15).

Finally, Moses and the Israelites approached the borders of the Promised Land. Moses sent twelve—one man representing each clan or tribe in the camp—to reconnoiter. Moses waited, longing to sweep triumphantly into Canaan.

The twelve spies returned. Two, Joshua and Caleb, urged an immediate advance and stated that the Israelites could find territory to hold. The majority, however, painted a frightening picture. The people were sullen and in no mood for heroics. They wanted to go back to Egypt.

Back to Egypt—back to the sluggish, half-human existence of slavery? What fools, Moses thought. How could they so easily desert the God who had so steadfastly refused to desert them?

Worse, however, was in store for Moses. Rebellion flared again. Once more, troublemakers began to hatch plans to murder Moses, grumbling that he was an unfit leader. An epidemic suddenly erupted, snuffing out the revolt. The people, however, cruelly accused Moses of causing the epidemic, of misappropriating funds, of using high-handed tactics. A split-off group actually made a foolish rush for the Promised Land, but, outnumbered and incompetently led, suffered total disaster. Moses agonized as the Lord's people seemed about to disintegrate into packs of snarling ruffians.

Moses' loneliness deepened when he suffered a series of deaths in his own family. The loss of his sister and his brother left him without the counsel of trusted relatives.

The journey seemed to stretch endlessly. The same problems

of morale and diet recurred with monotonous regularity. When the Israelites finally, painfully brought themselves almost within sight of the edge of Canaan, the ruler of Edom refused to allow them passage through Edomite territory. This meant another exhaustingly long detour. Instead of traveling up the regular caravan route to Canaan, the Israelites were forced to go far out of their way, plodding through barren, uninhabited stretches of jagged stones and shifting gravel, where poisonous vipers and bad water took a terrible toll.

For Moses as for everyone else, the thrill and romance of being God's pilgrims sputtered out. The dreary years in the desert burned out the dreams of their youth and the plans of their manhood. Thirty-eight years had passed since Moses had threatened/coaxed the Israelites from Egypt.

More than anything, Moses wanted to cross the Jordan River and enter Canaan with his people. There, he knew, they would establish a pilot community for God, a working model of how God intended people to live. Moses, tempted frequently to wash his hands of the ungrateful Israelites and quit, became almost obsessed with crossing the Jordan. On many nights, worn out by the gripes and problems, he wearily told himself, "Wait until we cross the Jordan; things will be different." He longed for the taste of victory, ached to accomplish his assignment and relax in Canaan.

After thirty-eight years of leading the Israelites through the desert, however, Moses began to have some nagging misgivings about whether or not he would get to Canaan. His strength began to wane. He felt the unmistakeable signs of aging—the vague aches in his joints, the constant tiredness in his chest, the dizziness when he got up or bent down, the problems of hearing and seeing clearly.

Moses prayed. In fact, he prayed several times about having enough strength to get across the Jordan. Moses' prayers turned into sleeve-tugging appeals: "Lord, I remind You that I'm counting on being around when You get this crew across the Jordan and settled in Canaan. I'm wearing down, God, but You'd better let me go across the Jordan."

When God seemed to indicate that He was not going to answer Moses' request, Moses pestered God even more. "Give me enough life, Lord, to get across the Jordan," Moses nagged.

God, it seems, turned down Moses. ". . . Speak no more to me of this matter" (Deuteronomy 3:26).

The closest Moses came to the Promised Land was a glimpse from the ridge overlooking the Jordan Valley. Then he died.

We all, like Moses, have our Jordans which we have never crossed—and never will. Everyone has tasks which are never finished, a promotion which never came, a career which never materialized, aspirations which never could be achieved. Like the little boy, tardy for school, who brought the excuse, "Please excuse Johnny; 8:30 came sooner than we expected!" all of us find that sixty-five comes sooner than we expected. And, in some cases, TOO LATE is stamped on plans for Promised Lands when we are twenty-one or thirty, forty or fifty.

That ridge where Moses got his look at the Promised Land is called Mount Pisgah, but it almost seems as if it should be called Mount Letdown.

Moses, however, learned to accept God's stiff "Speak no more to me of this matter," and, eventually, to live both gracefully and gratefully with God's answer.

But Moses, like most of us, arrogantly assumed that the progress of the planet would stop when he died. Like us, he conceitedly thought that everything in Israel rose or fell on his puny strength.

We, too, sometimes think that God's plans come to a halt when we decline or die. Part of our pride, our sin, is in wanting to be like God and exist forever. This refusal to accept our humanity tempts us all. We must be reminded that only God is immortal. We need to remember that for our good, He, *the* Eternal One, puts limits on our strength and on our days.

Moses also understood immediately that he was to coach Joshua as his successor. "Charge Joshua, and encourage and strengthen him; for he shall go over at the head of this people, and he shall put them in possession of the land . . ." (Deuteronomy 3:28).

Being part of God's people is like running on a relay team. One, then another, advances the baton. Each runner holds it for one lap. Each receives the baton from another, carries it briefly, then relinquishes it to a teammate. Each knows also that team victory is what is most important.

In God's work, each of us is responsible for maximum effort during the brief span allotted to us, our lap in life's race. Each of us has received the precious burden of powers, but each ultimately must relinquish these to others. God intends that we accept, use, and share whatever we have been given.

Moses was given a glimpse of the Promised Land. That was enough. He received evidence of the future.

Our God's solemn word has been given that He completes what He begins. He intends to carry out His plans. Through Jesus Christ, He discloses that the new society in which He intends everyone to dwell is to be made known by His caring community. When you and I help advance that promised society in the confidence of knowing God's ultimate triumph, we will have lived as fully as we can!

3

Joseph,
who was tempted to have an affair

She gave Joseph a warm smile.

Joseph returned her smile. It felt good to be appreciated. It particularly felt good to be appreciated by the boss's wife. Joseph recalled that very few people had appreciated him. Certainly not his brothers, who had sold him as a common slave that fateful day back in Canaan. Nor had the Ishmaelites, the rough traders who bought him from his brothers and dragged him from the home and family which he knew he would never see again. And the Egyptians certainly had not appreciated him— not the way they had herded him through the filthy slave market and subjected him to the indignities of being peddled like a work animal. Yes, Joseph assured himself, it almost restored his sense of being a human being to have Potiphar's wife smile at him.

In spite of the rough breaks he had experienced since being torn from home, Joseph had refused to quit. He worked hard for Potiphar, his master. Joseph, a strapping, energetic young man in his late teens, quickly won the respect of Potiphar. Furthermore, Joseph showed that he could be trusted. Joseph felt grateful when his Egyptian owner, Potiphar, recognized his long hours and attentiveness and gave him more responsibility. Eventually, Joseph had charge over all of Potiphar's personal and business affairs. Joseph looked after Potiphar's interests as if they were his own.

Potiphar, commander of the Pharaoh's elite palace guard,

rewarded Joseph generously. Potiphar's duties took him away from his lavish estate often, and he was relieved that he could leave his household staff, his properties, his investments, even his checkbook, in Joseph's competent hands.

Potiphar's wife often smiled at Joseph. Joseph always smiled back, and felt glad that even Potiphar's wife seemed pleased with his work.

Joseph noticed one day that Potiphar's wife was watching him. The husky, handsome, young Hebrew wondered why she was eyeing him. When he looked at her questioningly, he was reassured at once that she was not acting in a hostile or critical way. Joseph liked her friendliness. And he, a slave boy, felt flattered that the master's wife would notice him.

During the next weeks, Joseph occasionally encountered Potiphar's wife glancing at him and beaming her warm smile. Joseph, busy with his duties and conscious of his station as a servant, courteously acknowledged her greetings. Secretly, he enjoyed the attention. Also, he knew that it helped to have the boss's wife on his side.

She began coming to Joseph often with questions, with incidental requests. He good-naturedly answered them all. Everyone likes to be liked and everyone needs to be needed; Joseph thrived under the gentle shower of interest and dependency shown by Potiphar's wife. After the searing experiences of being shackled and peddled by his brothers, almost collapsing each day under the pitiless sun during the grueling march, being reduced to the nonperson existence of a common slave, Joseph found himself refreshed by her little attentions. He appreciated the way in which she seemed to instill a sense of manhood into him again. He did not feel like a slave or a functionary when Potiphar's wife asked him to do something for her. He cheerfully obliged, grateful to repay the favor of her interest in him.

Joseph, Potiphar's wife had observed, was totally unlike any other slave she had come across. The rest had usually been shifty-eyed sneaks, furtively engaged in a constant round of petty thievery. Or they had been lazy dullards who never seemed to get instructions straight and who could usually be found snoozing behind a shady wall. Threats and thrashings seemed to make little difference; none of them ever performed satisfactorily. This handsome Hebrew lad, however, handled himself so differently, she realized. His good manners and flawless honesty marked him as more than one born in the serf caste.

With her husband, Potiphar, out of town so often on government business, the woman found herself drawn to the virile-looking young slave for conversation. She discovered that Joseph had an astonishing maturity for his years. His wit and intelligence made him an engaging talker. At the same time, she noticed that he showed a refinement and gentility which she admired.

She also detected that Joseph always had a slightly disconcerting way of putting business first. Several times, she felt mildly hurt when he excused himself to return to his duties. Why, she wondered, did Joseph always seem to insist on tending to work? She wished that she could have longer talks with Joseph. She sometimes wondered if she could have his undivided attention for more than an occasional half hour of chitchat.

One day, after they talked lightheartedly for a while, Potiphar's wife slowly brushed her hand across Joseph's as he prepared to leave. Joseph was startled. He had never had any woman touch him before. He turned around, not sure of the meaning of her touch, not sure of his own emotions.

He looked at the face of Potiphar's wife. He read a tenderness and a softness in her expression.

After an awkward pause, Joseph's good-looking face widened into a broad grin. They both laughed. Joseph gracefully waved, turned, and went out.

Joseph had sensed biological urges in a vague way many times previously, but he had never focused his sexual feelings on any partner up until then. As a hardworking kid back in Canaan, he had been too young and too busy. He was only seventeen years old when his brothers trussed him up and turned him over to the caravaners who marched him to Egypt. Since then, there had never been any occasion for heeding the powerful drive he as a male in the peak of potency felt.

After Potiphar's wife touched him, however, Joseph became more sharply aware that he was a man with strong sexual stirrings, a man who could respond profoundly to a woman's caress, a man who had a deep primal desire to embrace. It awed Joseph, even frightened him. He tried to busy himself to the point of exhaustion, but he lay awake that night for a long time thinking.

The following day, he laughed to himself that his fantasies and feelings of the previous day were boyish silliness. Besides, he reminded himself, he had work to do.

The next few times when Joseph met the woman, it was so innocent, so free of innuendos, that he privately chided himself for giving way to thoughts of passion that time when she had touched him. When she had apparently caressed his hand, he insisted to himself, it was accidental, and it meant nothing.

Some weeks later, when they happened to meet, Joseph was overseeing the work of some of the staff of gardeners. Joseph, occupied with instructing the groundskeepers, had not seen the woman approach. Hot and weary from a long morning supervising a work crew under the enervating sun, the Hebrew lad nonetheless gave crisp orders and kept the men moving. Joseph was surprised to see the boss's wife standing nearby.

"You look like you need something cool," she said softly.

Joseph smiled and wiped his sunburned face.

"Come inside," she invited. "It's time for the midday break anyhow."

Joseph dismissed the workmen, threw a light tunic over his strong, browned shoulders, and obediently followed her into the house.

The Hebrew youth felt deeply flattered when Potiphar's wife insisted on serving him refreshments in person. It heightened his sense of self-esteem and masculinity to be waited on by the wife of his master.

Joseph savored the cool drink. He relaxed in the comfortable furniture. After a hectic morning in the heat, he felt pleasant and drowsy.

"It's time for the afternoon siesta," the woman announced.

Joseph nodded.

She quietly glided over to Joseph. Reaching down, she took his hands in her hands and gently urged him to his feet.

Fire raced through Joseph's body. He looked down at her.

Desire seemed to radiate from her entire body. Still holding Joseph's hands, she took a step backward.

Joseph, tingling with the tug of her hands on his, followed a pace.

Potiphar's wife quietly let Joseph's hands fall, and softly placed her fingers against the neckline of Joseph's tunic. Her face tilted upward, close to Joseph's. Tenderly, she whispered, "Lie with me" (Genesis 39:7).

Joseph throbbed with passion. A few steps beyond was her bedroom. They were alone. No one could disturb them. Indeed, no one would know. Potiphar was away and would never suspect anything. She was willing, even pleading.

Joseph's body demanded that he continue. His glands pumped powerful chemicals into his bloodstream which churned furiously through his brain.

"Go on," his impulses screamed. "Why not? I'm entitled to some fun. About time I have some kicks, do my own thing. I've been missing out. . . .

". . . Besides, everyone else does. This is the single swinger's life-style! This is easygoing Egypt; this is today! This is where I live, not the straitlaced, Hebrew small town of years ago! Live it up now. Who knows, tomorrow we all may be dead.

". . . Enjoy! Why wait? Why repress those feelings? Restraints are unhealthy and old-fashioned.

". . . And why should I disappoint her? It's her idea!

". . . Why not go along with her? Just this once. If I don't, she may make things rough for me!

". . . As long as no one gets hurt, anything is okay. And we're not going to hurt anyone. Just going to have a little fun, that's all."

God, however, firmly said *no!*

Joseph clearly understood that God forbade him to go to bed with Potiphar's wife. Joseph realized that God does not mumble, *Maybe, in certain situations.* He knew that God does not wink and shrug, *Boys will be boys.* Joseph accepted God's set of limits. Regardless of Joseph's feelings, regardless of the context, Joseph grasped that God's answer was—and always will be —a blunt negative to any affair with Potiphar's woman or any other except the woman to whom Joseph would commit himself for keeps.

Joseph bit his lip. He tried tactfully to tell Potiphar's wife that he could not break trust with Potipahr. After all, Joseph explained, "My master has no concern about anything in the house, and he has put everything that he has in my hand; he is not greater in this house than I am; nor has he kept back anything from me except yourself, because you are his wife . . ." (Genesis 39:8,9).

Joseph pleaded that he would be acting irresponsibly, that he would be hurting Potiphar. This, Joseph added, was something he could not do, something God would not permit.

The woman lowered her gaze. She murmured that she understood. Demurely looking up again at Joseph, she whispered that she respected Joseph immensely for his standards. She quickly walked away and closed the door to her room.

Joseph felt drained. Although he accepted God's command, he wondered if he would be able to withstand the temptation to have an affair if it should arise again.

The temptation did arise—and soon. The following day, at siesta time, she invited him to join her for lunch. Afterward, she went toward her bedroom and paused at the door for several seconds. Looking at Joseph, her pose and expression communicated an unmistakable invitation.

Joseph excused himself.

He resolved not to allow himself to be alone in the house with Potiphar's wife. His resolution was seriously challenged, however, every time she found him. He noted that she was inventing excuses to speak to him in the garden or at his desk. Although she pretended to want to talk about household matters, he knew that she really was trying to convey another message.

Joseph maintained a pleasant politeness with her. Inwardly, he felt the tug-of-war raging between the pull of God and the pull of his libido. Each day, he prayed for strength. But he wondered how long he could continue to withstand her appealing assaults on his standards.

One day, the woman approached him and suddenly started to cry. Impulsively, Joseph started toward her to comfort her. He checked himself. God's *no* again seemed to ring like a warning gong somewhere in his mind. She took her hands away from her tear-stained face, looked pleadingly at him, and sighed, "Oh, Joseph; Oh, please!"

Nearly weeping himself, Joseph rushed away. He made up his mind that he would have to be more careful so that they would not be alone under any circumstances.

Each day called for prudent planning so that he would always be with some of his staff. It took extra time and it demanded frequent schedule changes. Joseph, however, determined that he would be faithful to God and responsible to his benefactor, Potiphar.

Some weeks later, certain that she had gone out for the morning, Joseph went into the house to tend to some business on Potiphar's desk. Joseph assumed that the servants would be also in the house as usual, and never suspected that Potiphar's wife had privately ordered them to stay out. Preoccupied with paper work, Joseph had no inkling of the trap.

Startled by a rustling noise behind him, he looked around. He saw the woman. He also noticed that she stood clad only in a thin robe, suggestively loosely fastened.

She moved toward him. Stretching out her arms, she took hold of Joseph's tunic. She turned her head slightly to one side and looked at him provocatively. Her sultry voice spoke Joseph's name with a come-hither tone.

Joseph flinched. He felt her fingers gripping his garment. He tried to step away as gently as possible. He felt himself clutched, almost as if by an enormous crablike creature. His face grew hot, and he could feel perspiration starting to ooze down his body. His throat tightened with anxiety, and he could not think of any words to say.

Her voice seemed hoarse and insistent, "Lie with me" (Genesis 39:12).

Joseph wrenched free, squirming out of his tunic. He left her holding it and fled. As he rushed from the room, he heard her screaming his name. Her shrieks—shrill, piercing cries of anguish—carried through the house and through the grounds. Joseph hurried outside.

He uneasily wondered if there would be further scenes with Potiphar's woman. He quickly learned, however, that virtue is not always rewarded.

Potiphar's wife, hysterically weeping, called in her houseboys and maids and screeched that Joseph had attacked her. Accusing her oft-absent husband of importing the Hebrew outsider to the household, she sobbed and screamed, "See, he has brought among us a Hebrew to insult us. . . ." She seized Joseph's tunic and held it up as the supreme bit of incriminating evidence. ". . . he came in to me to lie with me, and I cried out with a loud voice; and when he heard that I lifted up my voice and cried, he left his garment with me, and fled and got out of the house" (Genesis 39:14,15).

When Potiphar returned home that evening, his wife had rehearsed her lie carefully. Potiphar, furious over his wife's report that Joseph had tried to rape her, immediately called his guards and had Joseph dragged off to prison.

Joseph spent the next thirteen years in an Egyptian dungeon. Although he lost his freedom, he had kept his integrity.

Joseph willingly accepted God's *no* to an affair with Potiphar's wife because he understood that it would break trust with Potiphar and with God. Such trust-breaking, in Joseph's words, was a "great wickedness"; it meant that Joseph would flaunt God, or, again in Joseph's words, "sin against God" (Genesis 39:9).

Because of God's profound faithfulness to us, we are called to be faithful to Him and to each other. Throughout the story of God's dealings with us, culminating in the Crucifixion and the Resurrection, we know God's concern for us. We understand His commitment to us; Christ's Crucifixion reminds us that God's commitment to us is a total commitment. Through the Risen Lord, we comprehend that God intends to be in community with us.

In the area of sex relationships, your relationship with your partner is to be the same kind as God's toward both of you. It is to be a relationship of concern, in response to His concern and a relationship of commitment—total, permanent commitment —because of His commitment to you. It is to be a relationship of community where not only the bed but all of life is to be shared with the other. Therefore, God says *no* to the affair, to the extramarital fling, to so-called trial marriage, to sleeping around.

Throughout the Bible, sex is understood to be more than a biological act or baby-making. The biblical view is that the joys of physical intimacy are part and parcel of all the intimacies— psychological, spiritual, emotional, and intellectual—between a husband and wife who share the responsibilities of life for keeps. This is why the Bible speaks of the profound relationship between husband and wife—including the sexual relationship —in terms of "knowing" each other. God reserves this pleasure for the man and the woman who give their word to Him and to one another and to the society around them that they intend to share all of life and mean to be responsible for one another for as long as the other is alive. God says a hearty *yes* to sex in this context.

Today's with-it generation is trying to repeal the Seventh Commandment. A few years ago, the question was, "Why wait for marriage?" Today it is frequently, "Why marriage?"

We merchandise nearly everything with the sex-sell. Even advertisements for lawn mowers and heavy industrial machinery feature provocatively posed, nubile girls. We are subjected to what Harvard sociologist Pitirim Sorokin once called "the continuous pressure of a gigantic army of omnipresent sex stimuli."

No wonder our youth think that sex is the center of human existence. Our culture presents sex merely in terms of kicks and thrills. The illicit affair is glorified. The swinging life is extolled. The extramarital romance is exalted. The tempting sexual dalliance is propagandized. The cheesecake chase is honored. Our young people learn well from our overeroticized society. "Monogamy is monotonous!" they solemnly believe. Unless titillated by the thrills of promiscuity, they have been made to think that they are missing something.

We latter-day Josephs and Egyptian wives before the Cross understand that God's commitment to us is not casual, nor is it for as long as may be convenient. It is covenantlike. God's commitment is permanent.

Therefore, we rule out all consideration for the temporary relationship; we repudiate the "as long as nobody gets hurt" liaison. A refusal to be committed to another for life denies real humanity to each other. Each uses the other like a disposable plastic carton.

To lonely singles like Joseph, to bored suburban wives like Potiphar's wife, to any confronted with the glamorous temptation of a bed partner not his or her spouse, the gospel also demands community. Sex has meaning when the entire community is considered, when one man and one woman, thinking of the welfare of everyone in society, are willing to announce publicly that they intend to dedicate their lives to each other's growth in and through every area in their lives.

God does not intend you to be a spiritual dwarf. He means for you to be a person who happens to be man or woman. Through Jesus Christ, He has conferred personhood on you. He has expressed His concern for you, He has committed Himself to you. He stands in community with you. Your deepest and most meaningful relationship with another will come only when you, in response to what God has done, agree to be the same to your husband or wife.

4

David,
who wanted to build a monument

Not build a place of worship? Not permitted to erect a great soaring temple to the glory of God?

David was crestfallen. He had planned that temple carefully. Mentally, he had laid it out so that he could picture its enormous walls and imposing towers. He could even visualize splendid processions moving through his temple's stately courts, chorusing his psalms.

Somehow, it did not seem fair that David could not erect a temple. Everyone agreed that he was a man after God's own heart (*see* I Samuel 13:14). Had David not faithfully fought for the Lord's causes? Had he not consulted with the Lord at each step in his career? Who but David would have spared King Saul on two separate occasions out of respect for God's anointed, although Saul had repeatedly tried to murder David? Had David not obediently been God's outlaw, hiding in caves, dodging Saul's patrols? And was David not also anointed as God's chosen? Everyone realized that he was anointed for more than forced night marches and thirsty bivouacs in the wilderness. Had David not revered God by refusing to reign as long as God's other anointed (Saul) was still alive? Had David not shown a respect for God by refusing to gloat when Saul finally met death? Had not David magnanimously looked after Saul's survivors? Had David not turned to God and prayed whether or not he should take the kingship? Building a temple seemed to be David's right. Even God's stalwart spokesman, Nathan, at first had agreed that David should have his dream.

David told himself that it was his right to build a temple to God. God should permit him this little touch of vanity as a reward for past services. David reminded himself that he was genuinely religious. His psalms, each a devotional jewel, revealed a man who thought often and deeply about the Lord. David felt miffed when Nathan reversed himself and reported that God turned down David's temple talk. The temple, David mused, was intended to honor God.

Furthermore, David felt guilty. He had just completed an elegantly elaborate palace for himself. Lolling in luxury, he noticed the Ark of the Covenant—the battered old box signifying the presence of the Lord—resting under a makeshift tent, tarps flapping in the wind. The contrast between his place and God's was embarrassing to David. It disturbed David that he should be installed in such comfort while the symbol of the covenant-making God should be nothing more than an old, wooden box with carrying poles, half-exposed to the weather amidst the weeds and rocks of a vacant lot. A temple would ease David's guilt pangs.

Moreover, David had sound political reasons for building the temple. The temple, he shrewdly sensed, would help cement together the two kingdoms which had entered into a shaky union under David.

David remembered vividly the enmity between the two former kingdoms. To overcome some of the hard feelings David, as the new king of the new kingdom, had shrewdly resolved not to settle in either of the former capitals. Instead, he had captured Jerusalem, the old Canaanite citadel which lay between Israel and Judah, threatening the unity of the new nation. Jerusalem was neutral. Neither Israel nor Judah could claim it. It stood geographically in the center of the new nation. No tribe could say that Jerusalem was its territory, hence David avoided showing favoritism. Everyone had a stake in the new capital.

The proposed temple would break down the deep lingering feelings of regionalism and tribalism. By bringing all worship to Jerusalem in the grandiose new temple, David knew that he would focus more attention on his new capital. The national religion of the two former kingdoms would be tied in with David's new kingdom if a temple were built.

Earlier, David had rescued the Ark of the Covenant at Kir-jath-Jearim, where it had lain half-forgotten during the turmoil of the past years. With ceremony and celebration, he had had it carried to his new capital. That move enhanced Jerusalem as the national seat for everyone, whether from the north or south. All that was needed was a great national religious shrine to house the Ark. The temple would provide a permanent center for worship. In the days of the old tabernacle, the tentlike shelter for the Ark of the Covenant, the worship center could be shifted too easily. The temple would keep the religion's headquarters securely located in David's royal city. To David, his temple would centralize government and cult in one safe place, away from the intrigues of dissident tribal leaders. More important, David believed that his temple would help restore the shattered unity of the confederated tribes by providing a rallying point for every descendant of Abraham. What better reason for building a temple?

David also had some personal reasons for wanting his temple. He was restless. A man of action, he needed a new project. If he were alive today, David would sing at the Met, pitch for the Mets, and run for president—all in the same week. Building the temple would provide an outlet for his immense energies and creativity; it would give him something he could throw himself into.

David mused that generations to come, standing in awe at the splendor of his building, would praise the builder. He sometimes found himself pondering the comments which would be made, such as "Wasn't David a wondrous ruler to have built such a colossal structure!" His temple, he sensed, would confer certain immortality on him. Those in the centuries of the future would remember him because of his temple.

Then, too, the first gray hairs were appearing; the ill-defined twinges were reminding David that he was growing older. He guessed that he could no longer bound up wilderness mountainsides in searing heat or march all night, followed by hours of hand-to-hand combat, as formerly he had done. His body passed on to his brain the hints that middle age was making its inroads. David felt an urgency to leave something permanent in the midst of the impermanence of his own life. What better than a temple? Unwittingly, David became victim to an edifice complex. He resolved that he would immortalize himself in stone.

Cherishing his plans for a great house for God, King David prepared to transfer his dreams to drawing board. Everyone— even the prophet Nathan—agreed that David's temple was a noble undertaking.

Not long after, Nathan returned with word that God turned down the proposal to build the temple. The news affected David like a defeat by the Philistines.

David would have attacked Nathan's word, but he knew Nathan's stainless-steel integrity. David understood that God said *no* to his intentions to build the temple in Jerusalem.

Everyone has a streak of David in his personality. Every person feels a compulsion to build some monument to himself or herself. For some, it may be only a marble mausoleum vault in an expensive cemetery. For certain women, their monument will be an exquisitely furnished house, each piece painstakingly selected and matched, so that every room is an enduring shrine to the refined taste and decorative skills of the hostess.

For certain men and women, their monument is a corporation, a business, a department, a territory. Put in charge of certain operations, awarded a title and given authority, any person may quickly start to erect a temple for his or her own ambitions and pride.

Kings and corporation people aren't the only ones who find it easy to start temples to their own egos. So do presidents and preachers. George Bernard Shaw, the witty Irish playwright, when asked in what age he would have preferred to have lived, unhesitatingly replied, "The Napoleonic." When asked why he would have liked the Napoleonic Age, Shaw answered, "Because only one man thought he was Napoleon then!" In our age, nearly everyone is inclined to build little empires.

Every parent is tempted to press, carve, and chisel the offspring's personality and accomplishments to glorify the parent. What Little League game does not have at least one father determined to achieve a touch of immortality through his son's athletic prowess? What dance recital does not reveal some mother projecting her own hubris through her daughter's ballerina slippers? Behind one swimming champion stands a couple secretly and vicariously erecting a temple of personal glory fashioned of Olympic medals, causing such strained relations and resentments that on one occasion, the swimmer dressed down his father at poolside for interfering too much.

King David learned what few of us would-be monument-builders to our own pride learn, namely that our egos expand horizontally and vertically. David discovered he wanted to build to call attention to himself.

George Washington was another who wisely recognized the allure of monuments to one's own vanity. In 1782, the victorious Continental Army, thoroughly disgruntled with its treatment by Congress, seethed with unrest. All ranks openly discussed making the enormously popular General Washington their king, removing Congress and instituting a monarchy. Colonel Lewis Nicola, one of Washington's oldest and wisest commanders, put in writing what everyone was talking about, and suggested a coup d'etat installing Washington as king for life. If the commander in chief had been receptive to Nicola's suggestion and the urging of a host of friends, Washington could easily have assured a successful revolt and the establishment of a kingdom with himself as the first ruler. Washington firmly rejected the temptation to build such a monument for himself. On May 22, 1782, he wrote a letter to Colonel Nicola in which he rebuked Nicola for such a suggestion, labeling it "the greatest mischief that can befall my country."

David discovered that the insidious thing about erecting a temple was that it seemed so sensible. What better idea, after all, than building a beautiful house of worship? Who could find fault with that? David found that he could mask his egotism marvelously in such an enterprise. He could twist the reason for wanting to build his monument so that he could pretend that the temple stood for noble purposes.

We monument-builders for our own glory can delude ourselves into imagining that our temples glorifying self are for a greater good, for charity, even for God! Like David, we can always rationalize any whim so that it can appear divinely directed.

King David and you and I need to be reminded that all monuments to our own pride are doomed. God sets limits on our ambitions. God puts bounds on our schemes for glory. All our temples to self are perishable and impermanent. Colonels, kings, and commoners alike must understand that each of us is but one puny, weak person, with extremely limited strength and with extremely limited time. Few of us, however, have the sagacity to digest this truism.

The story has been handed down from early Greek times that a certain king commissioned the wisest man in his realm to reduce all human wisdom to one short, pithy phrase which would be completely true under every circumstance. The king emphasized that the words had to be suitable for every situation and for everyone and for everything, and were to be a distillation of all human knowledge so that they could be inscribed on a plaque hanging around the neck of the philosopher. The king waited. The philosopher pondered. Finally, the wise man reappeared before the king. On the plaque was an inscription which satisfied the king's requirements: AND THIS, TOO, SHALL PASS AWAY.

The Bible agrees, except to add, "But the word of the Lord endures for evermore" (1 Peter 1:25 NEB).

David became aware that his monuments and temples, his schemes and dreams would all, too, pass away. He considered this in several of his hymns.

> . . . we are dust.
> As for man, his days are like grass;
>   he flourishes like a flower of the field;
> for the wind passes over it, and it is gone,
>   and its place knows it no more.
> But the steadfast love of the Lord is from everlasting to
>   everlasting. . . .
>
> Psalms 103:14–17

Significantly, Jesus Christ's only monument was a cross. The symbol of failure, however, has become the emblem of victory. Because of the One who cared nothing about building for Himself, we learn that to give is to live. We discover that "In the cross of Christ I glory/Towering o'er the wrecks of time . . ." only His kingdom endures. All other empires, shrines, temples, and monuments totter and collapse.

Ultimately God says *no* to all our attempts to commemorate our own prestige. He has no use for our efforts to memorialize ourselves. He turns us down every time we beg to enshrine our own kingdom or power or glory.

Suppose you were to wake tomorrow morning and read your obituary in the paper. What monument would the community report that you had built? A temple to your own conceit? A shrine to your ambition? A memorial to your pride? A house for your glorification?

You, who are meant to be part of God's family, are one of the community of the Crucified One. You, too, must crucify self. Forget your ego trips. Abandon your monument-building. Trust Him, not yourself.

He who heads the community of the crucified, God's family, frees you from your paranoid concern to achieve immortality through your own efforts. He builds your life toward others, thereby making you a living monument for Him!

5

Elijah,
who wanted to quit

A recent Gallup Poll of clergy reported that 33 percent of all Protestant pastors have thought of resigning at some time. Likewise, according to the same poll, 23 percent of all Roman Catholic priests and 43 percent of all Jewish rabbis have at one time or another considered quitting.

Hearing these statistics, one aroused churchman exclaimed, "What's wrong with these guys? I didn't think men of God were supposed to quit."

Sometimes, however, even the most stalwart believer becomes demoralized enough to think of laying down his commission. Elijah, at one time, was such a man.

He had worn himself out in the Lord's work. Elijah did not mind getting tired, but he thought he should see some results.

He had pitted himself against the corruption in his nation and had worked without letup to reverse the rush to moral ruin. The problem, however, lay in that Elijah was fighting city hall, and city hall in this case was the notorious Jezebel.

Jezebel, daughter of the powerful ruler of the Phoenician city-state of Tyre, had been raised to get her own way at all costs at all times. Jezebel had also been raised as a fanatic devotee of Baal, giver of fertile farmlands, and Asherah, goddess of the sea. Her marriage to Ahab, monarch of Israel, was arranged as political alliance between Tyre and Israel. Jezebel shrewdly stipulated that she be allowed to bring her own religion with her when she moved from Tyre.

Accustomed to imposing her will on everyone, Jezebel
quickly brought Ahab to heel. She sneered at the unbending
moral views of the Israelite religious leaders. When her husband, Ahab, made a few gestures toward defending his ancestral faith, Yahwism, Jezebel soon intimidated both him and
most of the Lord's defenders into embarrassed silence. She
scoffed at the rigid sexual code of the Israelite people, labeling
them the equivalent of puritanical peasants. What Israel
needed, Jezebel decided, was the excitement and enlighten-
ment of an up-to-date outlook, fostered by the Baal-Asherah
cult. Jezebel determined to stamp out what she regarded as
stuffy, outmoded traditions. Her Israelite capital, Samaria, she
decided, would be a top attraction shrine for a faith that was
fun. She imported four-hundred-fifty Baal prophets. She built
an elaborate temple. Jezebel even convinced her husband to go
along with her so that ". . . Ahab served Ba'al a little" (2 Kings
10:18).

Jezebel's cult, a corrupting combination of superstition and
sex, quickly caught on. In spite of protests by some of the Lord's
spokesmen, many in the population found Baalism fascinating.
After all, it was officially sanctioned by the royal family. Furthermore, many had always had misgivings about giving exclusive allegiance to the Lord. It made sense to many Israelites to
hedge their bets—to compromise a little by respecting other
religions, especially when it was claimed that other deities regu-
lated the rainfall which made the crops grow and controlled the
reproduction processes by which the livestock birthed their
young. "Ignore Baal and Asherah," many said, "and your barley
won't sprout and your sheep won't lamb." And, undeniably, a
cult accentuating raw eroticism and providing prostitutes as
part of worship could not help but have popular appeal. The
farm boys from the hill villages of Israel had never encountered
anything like Jezebel's new religion. When the exotic foreign
queen denounced Yahwism as prudish and narrow, many Israelites laughingly agreed.

Elijah, a onetime farm boy himself, from the hill village of
Tishbe in Gilead, worried over the impact of Jezebel's depraved
cult on the young men and women of Israel. It grieved Elijah

to see the pride of his nation—the youth—lured from Yahwism and sucked into the character-destroying practices of Baalism. Unless Jezebel and Ahab were stopped, Elijah knew that the young people—the hope of the future—would be brainwashed by the blend of self-indulgence and superstition masquerading as religion. Faith in the living God, Elijah shrewdly surmised, was only one generation from extinction.

Elijah felt a deep concern about the Israelite youth and how they were being seduced and degraded by Jezebel's mod gods. Elijah also grew perturbed that Israel, God's people, was fast forgetting its divine destiny by consorting with Jezebel's cult. Elijah knew that Israel was intended to be different from Jezebel's Tyre and all other nations. Israel, Elijah remembered, had been brought into existence by the Lord. Israel, Elijah recalled, was meant to carry out the Lord's plans.

Elijah correctly saw that Israel was not only degenerating into another minor sex-and-magic-obsessed power, but was failing to be God's special witness. Elijah churned with dismay and frustration as he watched Baal and Asherah erode the moral fiber of Israel and its people. Inwardly, he wept bitterly as he realized that his country was turning away from its God-selected identity and mission.

Elijah boldly criticized King Ahab for dabbling in Baalism while affecting outward forms of allegiance to Yahweh. Elijah guessed that Ahab's practice of giving his children Yahwistic names (Ahaziah, Jehoram, and Ataaliah were formed with the divine name *Yahweh*) was merely a bow to tradition, a sop to the old faith, a PR stunt for the masses. With words which stung like whiplashes, Elijah boldly denounced his ruler for "limping with two different opinions" (1 Kings 18:21).

When a prolonged drought scorched the land, Elijah seized the opportunity to force a showdown between Yahweh and Jezebel's cult. God's spokesman boldly challenged Jezebel's eight-hundred-fifty false prophets to a fire-building contest to decide once and for all whether the Lord or Baal was God.

The entire nation was invited to watch the proceedings. Elijah determined to prove to everyone that the Lord reigned supreme. He laid down dramatically simple terms. Two altars were built, one for the Lord and one for Baal. Firewood and sacrifices were placed on each. Elijah stated that he would call on the Lord to ignite the fire on his altar and demanded that priests of Baal and Asherah summon their deities to kindle the wood on their altar. Whichever deity answered, Elijah announced, should be accepted as supreme. Elijah then stood aside and invited Jezebel's hired holy men to have their gods produce fire.

Israel never forgot that day. *Mount Carmel,* the perfect setting for the contest, means the garden spot and is a great headland jutting out into the sea. Appropriately, Mount Carmel served as a favorite worship center for Baal, the provider of fertility, and Ashera, his sensuous consort. From early morning until noon, Jezebel's team of eight-hundred-fifty Phoenician prophets danced desperately around their altar, pleading with their deities to send down fire. They screamed in frenzy and whirled until they fell into dizzy ecstasy. When Elijah taunted them with failure, they hysterically shrieked and slashed each other with lances and swords. Finally, the prophets of Baal retired, defeated and exhausted.

Elijah stepped forward. In contrast to the frantic violence of the Baal prophets, God's man stood with a serenity and dignity which reflected his trust in God. Elijah asked that water be poured on the Lord's altar. Then he prayed.

Yahweh justified Himself that day on Carmel. It was the Lord's lightning, not Asherah's, which crashed down and consumed the sacrifice. It was God's rain, not Baal's, which poured down in sudden intensity, breaking the drought.

Elijah was hero for the day. Even King Ahab cringed before God's spokesman and carried out Elijah's orders. The cloud burst continued and the bystanders suddenly seemed baptized with fervor for their ancestral faith. The Israelites raced down Mount Carmel after the four-hundred-fifty Baal prophets and the four-hundred Ashera prophets and ruthlessly slaughtered every one of Jezebel's cult leaders.

Elijah exultantly believed that the Lord had been vindicated and the nation had been saved. Jezebel's corruption and debauchery apparently had been checked. The Baal-Asherah cult

had been wiped out. Elijah even hoped that Ahab would insti-
tute a reform movement which would bring Israel back to God.
As he waded through the surging waters of the flooded brooks
and hurried through the quagmire of the wide plain below
Mount Carmel, Elijah felt a mixture of fatigue and triumph. He
covered the fifteen miles from Carmel to the city of Jezreel
without stopping.

When he arrived in Jezreel, Elijah looked forward to a good,
hot meal and a long, well-deserved rest. He felt exhausted. The
rigors of the preceding months' preaching and protesting had
been physically and emotionally wearing. The events on Mount
Carmel, although finishing in an exhilarating victory, had also
worn down Elijah. The long slog through the rain and mud to
Jezreel had demanded what seemed to be the last reserves of
his strength. Elijah, however, assured himself that it all had
been worth it. The incredible investment of his energy had paid
off. Israel seemed secured for the Lord once more. Baalism had
been vanquished. Elijah felt a great sense of relief and accomplishment. He could relax and take it easy now. He could begin
to think of some of the other items on his personal agenda which
had been tabled during the long strife with Asherah and Baal.

Elijah had barely kicked off his sandals when a royal messenger banged on the door and curtly presented himself. The messenger announced that he had been sent by the queen, who had
just heard what Elijah had done to her eight-hundred-fifty cult
leaders. Elijah felt his stomach knotting as he heard how furious
Jezebel was. Jezebel, the messenger reported, decreed that
Elijah must die. A squad of killers was on its way. They would
assassinate Elijah in the same way the prophets of Baal had been
slaughtered. Within twenty-four hours, the messenger arrogantly stated, Elijah would be dead.

Elijah felt weak and half sick. From close study of Jezebel, he
knew how cunning and cruel she was. The messenger's words,
Elijah realized, were not idle threats.

Elijah quickly surmised that Ahab had spilled the story of the
Mount Carmel contest to Jezebel, but had weakly acquiesced
when his enraged queen screamed that Elijah and Yahwism
must be eliminated at once and Baalism reintroduced stronger

than before. Bitterly, Elijah recalled the king's professed awe at
the Lord's acts only a few hours earlier. Ahab, Elijah remembered, had meekly acknowledged Elijah's victory and had assured Elijah of his loyalty to God.

Where were all the cheering crowds now, Elijah wondered.
Thousands of Israelites had stood beside him after the Lord sent
down the fire on Mount Carmel. A few hours later, not a man
lifted a finger to defend him from the wrathful queen. Elijah
pondered the irony of the situation: from the Man of the Hour
to Public Enemy Number One; from Defender of the Faith and
Saviour of the Nation to the worst threat to the country's future
—all within one short day!

Elijah tried to keep himself from panicking. Too tired to think
or plan carefully, he could only feel anger and anxiety producing disjointed, disconnected images in his mind. With frightening vividness, he visualized Jezebel's paid assassins hurrying
through the dark streets, clutching their curved daggers under
their cloaks, breaking in on him, jabbing him with a series of
well-placed thrusts, and pitilessly leaving him to bleed to death
like a wounded animal.

The adrenaline surged and Elijah quickly stood up and
stepped through the door into the night. Flee! Leave Jezreel!
Get away from Jezebel's killers! Gripped by a primitive impulse
to save himself, Elijah flung himself through the deserted
streets. He passed the startled, sleepy watchman, let himself out
through the tiny emergency exit in the town gate, and ran.

Although exhausted by his day on Mount Carmel and the
fifteen-mile marathon run to Jezreel, Elijah hurried down the
Jordan valley, fleeing for his life. His only companion was a
faithful servant. The frightened prophet and his servant kept
moving throughout the night and the next day. Periodically,
after daybreak, Elijah peered back over his shoulder to see if
anyone was following. He suspected that Jezebel's secret police
were swarming throughout the kingdom, and were picking up
his scent. The humid heat of the steamy Jordan Valley grew
oppressive. Elijah, passing through the lowest part of the earth's
surface, longed to stop. His body pleaded for rest. Determined
to pass beyond the boundaries of civilization, Elijah pressed on.

He crossed into the southern kingdom of Judah. Still refusing to halt for more than quick breaks, Elijah kept moving at a fast pace until nightfall, when he and his companion holed up in a cave to snatch a few hours' sleep.

Even when they finally reached Beersheba, far to the south, Elijah still did not feel safe. He feared yet the cold steel of the blades of Jezebel's assassins. Leaving his servant, who by this time was so worn-out that he was useless and helpless, Elijah pushed on alone. The man of God advanced deep into the forbidding wilderness of Sinai. By the end of a long day's walking across the flint-sharp stones where the temperatures soar well above one hundred degrees Fahrenheit under the blinding sun, Elijah could proceed no farther. He staggered up a dry creek bed and collapsed under a broom tree. The broom tree in the *wadi* was merely a large shrub whose stick branches gave pitifully poor shade from the merciless sun, but to a man who had reached the end of his resources, it meant shelter. Elijah was finished.

Physically and emotionally spent, Elijah wanted to quit. Nothing mattered anymore. His commission as a spokesman for God? What difference did that make? How absurd human existence seemed! Even his own life no longer counted for anything.

Demoralized and defeated, Elijah dictated his letter of resignation to God. "It is enough," he croaked. "Now, O Lord," the onetime hero of Mount Carmel gasped, "take away my life!" Too weary to sob, Elijah wheezed that he was one more frail failure. His career would close with a death in the desert, and within a few days his bleached bones, picked clean by jackals and vultures, would be part of the forgotten dust of Sinai. He sighed that death had caught up with him, as it had with his father and his grandfather and *his* father. "I am no better than my fathers" (1 Kings 19:4), Elijah grimaced.

Sometimes, like Elijah, you are ready to quit. There seems to be no point in continuing. Your ambitions outstrip your abilities. Your friends let you down. Even God seems to back out, leaving you vulnerable and alone. Where are the victories? Why be a sucker, wearing yourself out for nothing? You feel disgusted with life, disgusted with yourself, disgusted with everything. The old words like *duty* and *discipleship*, which you once swore by, now seem hollow. Depressed and weary, you are at the point of resigning your commission from God.

God states a firm *no* when you or Elijah tell Him that you are quitting. The Lord refuses to allow us to drop out.

God's *no* to Elijah was communicated in ways both ordinary and extraordinary. First, God insisted that Elijah get some food and rest.

God knows that we are not disembodied spirits. He is aware that we have mundane needs, including bread and blankets, medicine, and money. The God who was so down-to-earth that He became enfleshed in a carpenter cares about bodies as well as souls. He has always had a profound interest in feeding, healing, helping. The God of the events in the Bible frankly has little in common with other religions because our God is not an idea or ideal to be speculated about, but the Activist-Doer who busies Himself with the nitty-gritty stuff of providing for the oppressed and hurting. God never loves in the abstract or with generalities; His care always appears in specific, concrete ways such as food or medicine. In particular, God communicates His concern specifically and concretely through bread and wine, just as He once completely spelled it out specifically and concretely in the earthly, flesh-and-blood episode of Calvary.

Bread and wine, penicillin and housing are still definite expressions of God's care. Often, the only vehicles to enable others to regain their trust in God and in life will be material, not spiritual. God's people who take their Bibles seriously quickly see the tie between God and the human needs of others.

Furthermore, Elijah's story reminds us suburban supermen that God intends for us to look after our own bodies. Premature coronaries and bleeding ulcers are not necessarily honorable badges of Christian service. The God who demanded that Elijah care for himself by getting sleep and food insists that we, His spokesmen and workers today, accept His gifts of rest and nourishment. Even Jesus took His disciples aside, saying, "Come away by yourselves to a lonely place, and rest a while" (Mark 6:31). Without occasional R and R leave, regardless of our zeal or commitment, we prove to be poor stewards of our health.

Part of God's answer to Elijah under the broom tree was an order to get some rest and take care of his body. Elijah began to get his confidence back after a long sleep and a hot meal—something Elijah had refused to take time for since fleeing from Jezreel. Part of God's answer to Elijah's plea to quit also came when God gave Elijah some of his own medicine.

Elijah had been a stern, tough thunderer. Elijah had shouted against God's adversaries. No gentle whisper of pity had been heard from him. He assumed that he was anointed to roar. Loud and angry, Elijah magnified God's strictness with a zeal which even God rejected. Elijah's only means of working with others were power and force.

Lonely for a sense of God's presence, Elijah endured a terrifying mountain storm. Hurricane-force winds shrieked and tugged at the hapless prophet. Earthquake tremors shook the mountain, breaking loose huge pieces of rock. A violent electrical storm followed, and lightning bolts crackled and crashed around Elijah. As the entire landscape shuddered in nature's frightening display of raw power, Elijah huddled in a crevice.

Elijah found no healing in the wrath of the storm. Instead, he knew nothing but terror. There was no comfort in the awesome might of the winds, the earthquake, and the fire. For Elijah, God was at best a primal force, terrible and impersonal.

Later, in the voice of gentle stillness, Elijah began to understand God's quiet presence. He learned that God handled him with a compassionate tenderness. Blustery Elijah got the message that he had been going at others the wrong way.

It's a world of snippy clerks, grouchy bus drivers, surly customers, and office bullies. Our usual reaction? Denounce! Threaten! Lecture! We itch to lay down the law—to set them right. All of us are brilliant at storming and censuring.

Significantly, God never shouts at us through a bullhorn, "Shape up or ship out!" Instead, He chooses to disclose His presence in a way of disarming gentleness. God's way is still the gentle voice, the compassionate word. He who could storm at us perseveres in loving us. Even when we insist upon consigning ourselves to our own destruction, He cries rather than rages. We can do no less.

After the wind, earthquake, and fire, God's voice in the soft

stillness asked, "What are you doing here, Elijah?" (1 Kings
19:13).

Although Elijah had been refreshed by food and rest, and
although Elijah had been tamed by his encounter with God in
the voice of quiet, Elijah still felt sorry for himself. He began to
recite his woes. Elijah related how zealous he had been for God,
and how wicked the people of Israel had been. With the moaning tone of one who thinks he's been badly used, Elijah told the
Lord how hopeless things were in the nation. All of God's
spokesmen had been slain, Elijah announced. "And I," Elijah
stated with the certainty of an accountant who has double-
checked his figures, "even I only, am left; and they seek my life,
to take it away" (v.14). Elijah felt that this statement clinched
his argument. How could God refuse to permit him to quit
when the odds were so overwhelming?

God told Elijah to stop trying to do the Lord's bookkeeping
for Him. Elijah's head count and the Lord's would never agree
anyhow!

Quit trying to tally the score, Elijah, God, in effect, reminded
His prophet. *Your ideas of success and failure and Mine are
different. You are always adding up numbers or looking for
immediate results! Forget it! Your job is simply to be faithful
and responsible, then to leave the final outcome to Me.* In so
many words, the Lord also reminded Elijah that there were
others who were also faithful. *Elijah, you think that you are the
only loyal person in the entire nation? Nonsense! Actually,
there are seven thousand faithful believers. But they need you
and you need them. Now stop complaining about how bad
things are and how tough you've had it. Enough of your talk
of quitting!*

God ordered Elijah back to work. "What are you doing here,
Elijah?" (v.13). A good question! Elijah was doing nothing except
telling himself how unfair everything was. Elijah was tamely
allowing one woman, Jezebel, to dominate Israel and overawe
him. "Go, return on your way to the wilderness of Damascus,"
God commanded Elijah (v.15). In other words, *Back to your
post! Resume your duties!*

Specifically, Elijah was told to do two things: to anoint a new king in Syria and another in Israel, and, second, to select Elisha as his successor as leading prophet. This was God's way of telling Elijah that he was to help shape the destiny of the nation and also to train the next generation to carry on God's work after him.

Once God refreshes anyone and shows His compassion, He insists on that person's returning to active duty. God says *no* to anyone who tries to retire to a mountain and sulk.

There is no permanent retirement for a Christian, only temporary respites from time to time to rest and reequip. Even when we try to go AWOL from Christian service, God gently but firmly turns these lapses into furloughs. He persists in recommissioning us. His answer to us would-be quitters is always a refusal, because His big plans include us!

6

Jonah,
who wished to get away from it all

"Go to Nineveh? To *those* people? *Never!*" Jonah snapped.

Jonah growled to himself that he had heard enough of crazy schemes like going to preach to people in Nineveh. Why were these Nineveh ideas always tagged with God? How could anyone be so sure? Whoever thought it up, and whatever the notion was, it was absurd.

What was the point in anyone going to Nineveh, Jonah wondered. He snorted. No one in Nineveh would listen if anyone did go on behalf of God. Nineveh, Jonah remembered, was the capital of the cruelest war machine in the world. Jonah assured himself that no one in Nineveh would give the time of day to any preacher. To go to Nineveh, Jonah convinced himself, would be a farce—a waste of time.

"Besides," Jonah argued to himself, "I'm free. Why do I have to go along with this evangelism nonsense if I don't want to? I'm tired. Tired of social activism, tired of missionary crusades, tired of causes—period! People think I'm some sort of fanatic always being told to dash off on this or that campaign. It's tough enough to be a believer in God without getting mixed up in Nineveh. I'm out of step enough without getting involved in the Nineveh problem."

Wearily, Jonah looked around him. What he saw bolstered his reluctance to dash off to Nineveh. "We've got plenty to do right here at home," he stated to his friends. "Look after our own before we tackle others' problems, I say!"

Secretly, Jonah was fed up with pressures of being told that he was responsible to others all the time. Furthermore, Jonah was not comfortable with Ninevehites. They were not like him; they were not his type, he felt.

Jonah confided once or twice to those closest to him that he was annoyed with the people from Nineveh because they never showed any sense of responsibility. "Let them show some sign of wanting to act decently," Jonah declaimed, "and I'll be the first to give them a hand. However, every time I pick up the newspaper, there is some new outrage by Nineveh! I've had enough of their upsetting everything—including me!"

Some of Jonah's buddies told him that he was working too hard and worrying too much. What Jonah needed, they insisted, was a good rest. "Get away from the pressures," they urged Jonah. "Take a nice, long cruise."

The idea appealed to Jonah. He had been driving himself rather hard, he assured himself. His nerves were shot. A change of scenery, a long-overdue vacation, a chance to get away from it all seemed to be just what he needed.

Jonah talked to his travel agent. When he heard about the slow boat to Tarshish, it suited his plans perfectly. Tarshish, Jonah dimly recalled, was the end of the line, the last stop on any transportation line, the farthest point he could go in the world. Jonah immediately bought his ticket and said his good-byes.

Jonah would not admit it, but he was actually taking a ship to flee from his responsibilities. A Tarshish cruise was a pleasant escape. Since he was going to run away, Jonah determined to do it in style and comfort. He toyed with notions of staying for a while in Tarshish. Perhaps he would find a hideaway inland nearby to settle down in. Maybe one of the ports of call enroute to Tarshish would be the kind of idyllic retirement place he had sometimes thought about in his reveries.

Jonah smiled with anticipation as he walked up the gang-plank to his cruise ship. At last he could find a little contentment and peace.

The snap of the sail, the bracing sea breezes, the gentle motion of the ship brought Jonah a sense of euphoria. He had not slept so soundly for years. Each day, in fact, he retired for a couple of long naps.

The farther he sailed, the more content Jonah felt. Jonah told himself that he had been silly to get so wrapped up in involvements like Nineveh. Sunning himself in an area on the after-deck which was sheltered from the wind, Jonah closed his eyes and relaxed. Never again would he allow himself to get upset about others, he promised himself. Whenever his mind thought it picked up any faint signals about God's concern for others, Jonah quickly smothered the beeps of conscience with grandiose but vague assurances that he meant well and wouldn't hurt anyone.

When he retired one afternoon for a long rest, landlubber Jonah had not noticed the ominous signs of dirty weather. He blissfully dropped off to sleep. The pitching of the vessel acted as a rocking cradle, making him slumber more soundly than usual.

The seamen, however, frantically worked to help the ship to wallow through the rapidly worsening weather. Rains pounded and gale-force winds plucked and tore at the rigging and mast. The seas heaved and churned so that the waves began to appear like surging gray mountains on every side. Old-timers among the crew muttered that this storm was the worst that they could remember.

Jonah, however, slept blissfully on. When he finally awoke, he saw others, crew and passengers alike, working desperately to keep the ship safe. Jonah refused to join them. "Let them fret and sweat. Not me," Jonah announced to himself. "I'm on vacation!"

Jonah had tried to escape responsibilities to Nineveh and to shipmates. He had granted himself a sabbatical from service. Turning his back on others, Jonah had unwittingly tried to turn his back on God.

Although Jonah shut God out of his thinking, God would not forget Jonah. The Lord still had plans for Jonah.

Jonah began to understand that the storm during his cruise was God's way of reminding Jonah of duty and its consequences. Jonah discovered that his disobedience had gotten a lot of innocent people in difficulty. In fact, rightly or wrongly, it began to appear that everyone—Jonah included—believed that Jonah was connected with their predicament.

The blunt seamen shouted that Jonah was the cause of the storm. Superstitious as most seamen still are, they growled that Jonah had hexed the voyage, and Jonah's deity must be displeased.

Jonah, remorse-stricken, realized that his God *was* displeased. Contritely, Jonah acknowledged that he had been the cause of everyone's misery.

Jonah finally saw that he would have to do something. He noted that the seamen, although unbelieving heathens, were saints compared to him because they were straining to save everyone. It was a losing battle, however, and Jonah realized that he would have to become involved personally. His faithlessness had gotten everyone into trouble. Jonah determined to try to fix things up.

Jonah still had no intention of going to Nineveh. He had no love, no pity, no interest in others. A grudging believer in God, Jonah still meant to avoid the Ninevehites. He decided to make a deal with the Lord to get himself out of a jam. As a heroic gesture to save the ship, he allowed his shipmates to pitch him overboard.

The name *Jonah* is the Hebrew word for a dove. A dove was the traditional symbol for Israel, just as the eagle is a symbol for the United States of America, or a lion for the United Kingdom, or a bear for Russia. The story of Jonah was recounted as a parable of Israel's disobedience. The tale of the prophet taking a ship for Tarshish stood as an early example of the theater of the absurd to communicate a message. The symbolism behind the story is blatantly obvious: God's people must be faithful and obedient.

Every believer has his Nineveh. Every congregation has its Nineveh. The church in every generation has its assignment which it does not want to accept.

"To *that* place? With *those* people?" we groan. "It's no use working with slum dwellers," we announce, turning away from some particular urban Nineveh God targets today, or we sigh,

"It's pointless sending missionaries overseas now," choosing to ignore an Asian or African Nineveh which God is passionately interested in. "Why waste time and money on youth programs for runaway kids and addicts?" we bark, forgetting that these may be the Ninevehites today which God means for us to be with.

Not only does every Christian and every congregation have its own personal Nineveh, they also have their own private Tarshishes. "Let's not get involved" is a one-way ticket to Tarshish. Tarshish stands for a cop-out. Much of the time, God's people belong to the First Church of Tarshish. In Tarshish, the prayer always runs, "Use me, Lord—in an advisory capacity."

Today where despair is so persuasive and pervasive, many opt for Tarshish via a highly privatistic life. The trend is toward buying a camper and a boat, taking off, and getting away from it all. Tarshish may be the vacation home to which many retreat for the weekend after trying to exist for five days.

"I'm merely surviving until I'm sixty, then I'll retire and do as I please," one alumnus of the church told his pastor. There are innumerable forms of the trip to Tarshish.

By stern measures, if necessary, God says *no* to all who try to run from responsibilities. God leaves no hiding places.

In the late 1930s, a weary and disgusted pastor took a ship to an obscure tropical isle. He knew World War II would soon erupt, and he intended to wait it out in safety and comfort. Writing to friends in Australia, he described his South Seas paradise as the perfect haven and advised them to flee and join him. His friends in Australia didn't hear of him again, but they did hear a lot about his island. It was called Guadalcanal.

God turns us down every time we take ship for any Tarshish. Sometimes we think how pleasant it would be to gather a few congenial friends and retreat permanently to a remote spot where we could live life on our terms, regardless of international crises, regardless of domestic turmoil.

A few years ago, a dozen families from Long Island determined to escape from nuclear disaster. These fugitives from fallout picked their haven with the aid of an Atomic Energy Commission map, which indicated mountains and air currents, and arranged to move to a town in California.

The map, however, did not show what the inhabitants of the California town knew: that a Titan missile base was being built in the area which made the town a prime target in the event of an attack. The townspeople were astonished that anyone would consider moving there in order to be safe.

God permits no escape to anyone, particularly in these days. Instead, He insists that we all deal as faithfully as we can with the world as we find it.

Just as Jonah tried to snooze contentedly through his crises on shipboard, sometimes today there is a phony peace of mind which comes from escaping—temporarily—the surrounding crises. Actually, such escape-induced euphoria is indifference. Any time that we feel comfortable because we feel we have achieved such a blissful state of contentment, we had better check to see that it is not merely because we are deserting our duties or are becoming oblivious to obligations.

There is a dangerous kind of contentment where we think everything is fine—when it is not. This was Jonah's problem.

God speaks a stern *no* any time we doze off from our duty to others. Sometimes, it takes something like a storm to get us to hear God's *no* to our disobedience. The rough times around us today may be God's way of rousing us to service.

We often think that what we do is no one else's business. However, in the complicatedly interlocking relationships between every member of the human race, the selfishness of one affects others. No sin is private. Passengers all on the same frail craft called Planet Earth, starvation in the sub-Sahara affects Scarsdale, and a Watergate weakens confidence and currency everywhere. And sometimes God must use drastic means to rouse us to responsibility. It took a terrible storm to shake Jonah out from his lethargy.

Out of concern, God wakens us to save us and send us back to our tasks. He finally shook us out of the stupor of selfishness at Calvary and the Resurrection.

Jonah's selfishness and disobedience nearly caused the ruin of a whole shipload of innocent people. He had thought that his pleasure trip was his own business, but learned that a voyage to

Tarshish had all sorts of social ramifications.

After being tossed overboard by the crew of the ship, Jonah found himself propelled to Nineveh via an enormous fish.

Some who read the biblical story of Jonah get hung up on the details of the fish story. The Hebrew text speaks of a sea monster, not a whale (there are no whales in the Mediterranean), and in the Near East lore, such a sea monster personified the powers of chaos, darkness, and death. The point of the story is not how Jonah survived in the stomach of the sea monster, but how God rescued Jonah to send him to Nineveh. Although Jonah had been swallowed up by destructive forces, God returned him to active duty.

Jonah, the reluctant prophet, finally went to Nineveh. Taking his stance in the most prominent part of the wicked city, he delivered the divine message of warning. "You people here in Nineveh have gotten away with murder," Jonah in effect intoned. "God has set a day of reckoning. In six weeks, you will see once and for all that you cannot flaunt the Almighty!"

After delivering his verbal bomb, Jonah retired to the edge of the fallout zone and waited the forty days for God to punish Nineveh. Jonah had been happy to show indignation and pronounce doom.

Jonah felt satisfied after rebuking Nineveh, and busied himself imagining what sort of destruction God would rain down on the evil city. Jonah made one fundamental error. He did not comprehend that God never uses anyone's pronouncements or preaching to bolster that person's pride. Instead, as Jonah learned the hard way, God uses those pronouncements and preachings to offer an opportunity for repentance.

Jonah shrieked that Nineveh was abandoned by God, dusted off his hands, and slouched by the sidelines waiting for the day of retribution.

Two surprises followed. First, Nineveh repented. Second, God did not destroy Nineveh.

Jonah was astonished. Nineveh turning to God? God showing mercy to Ninevehites? Jonah grew angry and bitter. He had not expected anything to happen. Furthermore, he had not wanted anything to happen!

Jonah put on the airs of a pious believer who had been wronged. With an aggrieved tone, Jonah even indulged in some fake praying. The dialogue was devoutly worded but the gist was that God had double-crossed him.

"You dirty Forgiver!" Jonah bitterly accused the Lord. "You switched plans and decided to show mercy! I might have suspected that You would go soft on Nineveh. You allow Yourself to be swayed by the whimpering pleas of these godless vermin. I keep my part of the bargain and come to this wicked hole, but You welsh out! You get to feeling sorry for these Ninevehites.

"Lord, it's not fair to me. Go on, Lord, be kind to these worthless Ninevehites. See if I care! Waste Your love on them when they don't deserve a thing. By all rights, You should let them suffer and get what they have coming to them! Let the Ninevehites be on the receiving end for a change.

"If you are going to be compassionate toward these irreligious atheistic Ninevehites, I'm through! I should have known it would turn out like this. I always suspected that You'd feel a streak of pity toward these no-goods. Well, Lord, if You want to love them, count me out! Leave me alone. I've had it with them —and with You, too! Amen." (*See* Jonah 4.)

Although he had finally—reluctantly—gotten himself to Nineveh, Jonah really had still not "gone" to the Ninevehites. His counterfeit prayer had been a combination diatribe and ultimatum. Yapping for punishment for someone else and pouting because of unfair treatment, Jonah discovered God made no reply.

Whenever anyone prays without understanding that God has compassion on all others, God has, in effect, been repudiated. Prayer will be empty. God's apparent silence and distance is a form of *no* to such praying.

Jaw clenched, mouth set, and eyes glowering, Jonah sulked. He made himself comfortable under the shade of a gourd vine and waited for the catastrophe which he secretly expected God would pull off after all. Surely, he assured himself, God would wise up to what the Ninevehites were really like. After all, Jonah reasoned, being God, He ought to have *some* wisdom. And if He was a just God, Jonah's logic continued, He would settle His accounts with Nineveh fairly and quickly.

Meanwhile, under the gourd vine, Jonah waged his cold war against his enemies. BETTER DEAD THAN RECONCILED was Jonah's motto. Ignoring the order to fraternize issued by the Commander in Chief, the peevish prophet hoped that the Ninevehites would revert to their old ways so that they would be certain to get their comeuppance.

The merciless sun beat down, and Jonah felt grateful for the umbrella of leaves of the gourd vine. He noticed, however, that the leaves began to shrivel early the following day, and discovered a worm eating the heart of the stalk, killing the vine.

Jonah grew incensed. Saddened that the gourd vine should perish, Jonah reproached God. Why, Jonah demanded, should a plant which was valuable to Jonah be allowed to die?

The Lord put Jonah in his place. "You pity the plant, for which you did not labor, nor did you make it grow, which came into being in a night, and perished in a night. And should I not pity Nineveh, that great city, in which there are more than a hundred and twenty thousand persons who do not know their right hand from their left, and also much cattle?" (vs. 10, 11).

Jonah could get emotional over a simple vegetable, but begrudged God His love for His children, whom He had fostered and cared for. Jonah had pity on a plant but was indifferent to a city of over a hundred thousand! Jonah felt mercy toward a gourd but was unwilling to have God be merciful toward humans. Jonah missed the lesson God intended; namely, that if Jonah could be saddened over the death of a vine, how much more would God grieve over the destruction of a city!

God unmasked Jonah's unreasonableness. The Lord gave Jonah a taste of what destruction was like.

Jonah, who claimed a unique standing with God, tried to evade his missionary responsibilities. He convinced himself that God's concern was limited to certain persons. And he heard God's loud *no* to his attempts at evasion and exclusivism.

God still replies in the negative to those who claim a special relationship, but try to escape from responsibilities, or fall into a narrow, ethnocentric outlook. God vigorously protests whenever His Jonahs in any generation try to confine His compassion to a select circle of self-anointed saints.

We dare not justify selfish, nationalistic policies by pleading our special relationship to God. ("We are godly, they are godless.") Moreover, we must listen intently to the divine question to the Jonah people today: "And should I not pity Nineveh [or Havana, or Hanoi, or Peking, or Moscow, or Washington, or your present address], that great city, in which there are more than a hundred and twenty thousand persons who do not know their right hand from their left?"

7

Job,
who demanded answers

Even the older men stood up when Job walked into a room.
Everyone respected Job.

Job had earned the deference he received. And not merely
because he was the wealthiest. Job was the leading citizen of the
community in every way.

The embodiment of the traditional success story, Job's pros-
perity reminded everyone what hard cash and lots of hustle
could do. More important, Job showed that achievement and a
bankroll meant responsibility. Job generously shared his time
and his money. He contributed to every charity. He served on
civic boards and committees. The walls of his den, festooned
with framed tributes, appreciation plaques, and pictures of tes-
timonial dinners, recorded what a community-minded citizen
Job was. It was an open secret that he was a soft touch for any
youngster needing a job or a family down on its luck.

Although a socially concerned, kind person, Job did not
parade his piety. Religion, to Job, was doing, not talking. He was
more interested in finding work for a poor widow's son than
listening to tedious sermons or splitting doctrinal hairs.

Moreover, the probity of his personal life matched his public
life. No breath of scandal, no whiff of shame ever clouded Job's
name. He was totally faithful to his wife. A model father, he was
raising a large family of lively, attractive youngsters to whom he
was devoted. His rectitude in business dealings won respect
even among his competitors. Job's reputation for honesty and

fair dealing carried throughout the area. Never had he been tainted with charges or gossip about bribes, kickbacks, overpricing, or shady dealings. "Big-hearted Job," he heard himself called; "never a mean streak in him."

Job enjoyed his role as Mister All-Around Personality and Local Celebrity. Each day he strode vigorously down the busy main streets acknowledging the respectful greetings, the minor accolades from everybody from city officials to street-corner vendors. Job recognized that he was known by nearly everybody. He took satisfaction in realizing that his opinions were sought, that his suggestions carried weight.

In the prime of life, Job walked with the physical vitality of a man who had always enjoyed perfect health and expected to be virile and robust for many, many years.

His children gave him great pride. The older ones, just finishing school and not yet married, had survived the crises of adolescence and showed immense promise. The younger ones, in spite of their loud voices and habit of tracking mud on the floor, made the home radiate with love and laughter. All the boys had discussed coming into the family business because of their admiration for their father. Job's happiness knew no bounds.

He relished the present. He also looked forward to the good days ahead. Job anticipated the time when his children would marry, when they would establish their own homes. In occasional reveries, he found himself thinking of family reunions, of games and stories with grandchildren, of private jokes and pet nicknames they would enjoy. "The golden years," Job reflected. Job also expected to be productive for many working years. Still young enough to appreciate challenges, yet established enough to be free of pressures to succeed and financial anxieties, Job rubbed his hands in anticipation of the decades to come. He expected to savor many comfortable days of solid achievements.

Then Job's entire world suddenly collapsed.

One day, a messenger staggered in, out of breath from hurrying, to report a dire catastrophe. Job's most valued and irreplaceable assets had been wiped out: desert raiders had swarmed through Job's extensive agricultural enterprises, killing the plowmen and carrying off the prize livestock.

Job, still trying to get the details of the disaster, was interrupted by a second messenger. This messenger, like the first, turned out to be the sole survivor. His report—that lightning had electrocuted all of Job's sheep herds and herdsmen except the messenger—spelled financial ruin.

Minutes later, a third employee, gasping and disheveled from a hurried trip, arrived to spill out still more bad news. The last of Job's property was gone. His camel herds, representing years of investment and attention, had been stampeded by another party of wild desert tribesmen. All of Job's men had been slaughtered, except the messenger, and the camels had been driven eastward toward the empty desert. Job suddenly was destitute. He had no property, no investments, no business, no credit. He had nothing except mortgages and debts, and no hope ever of paying off these. Furthermore, Job had no possibility of starting over again. He knew that he was financially destroyed. Grimly, he shook his head at the swiftness of his losses. Yesterday, he had sat proudly as the community's most prosperous businessman. Today, he was no better than a beggar. Broke. Bankrupt. Finished. Job wondered how his wife and children would react to being reduced to living like paupers.

The next news came like a gigantic hammer blow. Job's children dead. All of them. Crushed when the house where they were all holidaying collapsed in a terrible hurricane. No survivors.

Too numb to cry, Job mechanically went through the motions of mourning. He knew that he had suffered irreversible losses and would have to exist in hopeless poverty the rest of his days. He told himself that he could accept that. But with his babies gone—his sons and daughters—he felt completely crushed. Being a beggar was bad enough, but a *childless* beggar seemed to be the final agony.

Not long after, Job noticed sores appearing over his body. To his consternation, he saw that they did not dry up and disappear. Instead, Job watched them turn into huge, ugly, oozing carbuncles. From the soles of his feet to his scalp, Job's flesh became a seeping mass of pus-filled infection. His skin cracked and seemed to turn into great blackened blotches of suppurating scabs. The gruesome sores even appeared in his throat, where their festering caused him to choke in his sleep. Sleep came hard because it hurt his pain-wracked body to have anything touch the sores. His back, sides, and chest had such deep, raging boils, that any time Job sat, leaned, or laid down, he gasped and groaned.

No medication brought relief. Job tried every remedy. Instead, his condition worsened.

His appearance changed so drastically that old friends did not recognize him. Youngsters in the street, many of them children of longtime friends, made fun of his gruesome sores and scab-covered body. As the disease made Job more loathsome looking, people began to avoid him. Even relatives and close friends, repulsed by the sight of the putrifying flesh, stayed away.

Job sensed that no one wanted him around. He became aware that he was already as good as dead as far as everyone in town was concerned. In fact, he could almost imagine them wishing that they could bury his still-breathing corpse.

Even his wife turned against him. Weary from tending her cranky, sick husband, and derelict herself from losing all her children, Mrs. Job advised Job that his case was hopeless. One night, after a particularly trying day with Job, she snapped that he should give up and renounce both God and life.

The man who had lost everything—children, possessions, health, and friends—realized that he had also lost a future. Job sank into the abyss of loneliness.

"My kinsfolk and my close friends have failed me. . . . I am repulsive to my wife. . . . Even young children despise me. . . . All my intimate friends abhor me," Job lamented, "and those whom I loved have turned against me" (Job 19:14,17,18,19).

Job was not patient. Nor was he pious. Instead, he cursed and raged. Thomas Wolfe correctly dubbed Job, "God's angry man."

When three sanctimonious friends stopped by, Job bitterly assailed the Lord. What was the point to human existence? Why such misery?

Job's words shocked them. His curses echoed with blas-

phemy. His questions challenged their dogmas. His unrepent-
ant attitude offended their orthodoxy. Fidgeting with irritation,
the three knew that they could not allow Job's grumbling to go
unanswered. Was it answers, explanations, reasons which Job
cried for? Very well, they would provide them.

Eliphaz, a fatherly type who had known Job since Job was a
boy, gently started to help Job see the error of his ways. God is
just, observed Eliphaz. God can find some fault in everyone.
Obviously, Eliphaz pointed out, because Job was having a hard
time, it meant he had some faults. Eliphaz, a well-intentioned
preacher, nodded sagely and quietly let his words sink in. Job
had offended God. Then, with an if-I-were-you tone, Eliphaz
advised Job to own up and come clean. If Job would seek divine
forgiveness, Eliphaz assured the miserable man, everything
would turn out nicely. Eliphaz concluded primly by issuing his
version of a little "altar call."

Eliphaz's words had a proper, pious ring, like poetry read
unctuously to the sobbing strains of organ music in a funeral
parlor. Job, however, remained unmoved. Confess his sins, and
everything would turn out nicely? To a man who had lost his
children, how could anything turn out nicely? Job sourly
growled, "Why doesn't God finish His jokes and kill me off?"

Recalling with bitterness the words of Psalm 8, "What is man
that thou art mindful of him, and the son of man that thou dost
care for him?" Job cynically rephrased the beautiful prayer.
"What is man, that thou dost make so much of him, and that
thou dost set thy mind upon him, dost visit him every morning,
and test him every moment?" (7:17, 18). Why did God delight
in testing him? With heavy sarcasm, Job chided the Lord for His
lavish attention to him. What had he done to deserve all this
misery?

Job's second friend, Bildad, decided that he had better step
in. Less considerate than Eliphaz, Bildad considered himself
something of a scholar. He had done some studying. Bildad had
researched the Great Thinkers and pondered theological doctrines and he believed firmly that evil deeds are always followed
by a penalty. He was also convinced that God constantly
watches the balance sheet of sin in everyone's life and insists on

settling accounts promptly with stiff penalties. *Justice* was the favorite word of Bildad, Job's dogmatic acquaintance.

Job wondered if God was as bad as Bildad's theology implied. If so, Job asked what was the use of pleading his case to God? How could anyone know if God listens or cares? "If I summoned him and he answered me," Job cried, "I would not believe that he was listening to my voice" (9:16). With bitterness, Job asked why God persisted in pronouncing him, an innocent man, guilty. "Though I am innocent . . . though I am blameless, he would prove me perverse" (9:20). Why, Job demanded, did God apparently laugh at the plight of a virtuous man like him? "When disaster brings sudden death," Job said, "he mocks at the calamity of the innocent" (9:23). How could God permit a man who had sincerely tried to lead a godly life to go through such torture? Why was God not on speaking terms with him?

Job plunged on. He demanded answers, but acrimoniously fired another volley of questions at God and at his three friends. What was the reason for God's assault against him? "Let me know," Job barked at the Lord, "why thou dost contend against me" (10:2). How could the God who was supposedly good, the One who created Job in the first place, cheapen the work of His own hands by injuring Job? Didn't God realize that this served to aid and abet the cause of the wicked? Was God a peevish ogre who took sadistic pleasure in hurting? "Thy hands fashioned and made me," Job reminded the Almighty, "and now thou dost turn about and destroy me" (10:8). Did the Creator have second thoughts about His creation? Job wanted to know. God, Job croaked, was more like a lion, ready to pounce on the unwary and helpless, attacking and maiming (*see* v. 16). What could the Lord gain by hurting him so badly, Job pleaded.

Zophar, the third member of the trio of "comforters," could not contain himself any longer. Zealous Zophar harshly screeched at Job to stop mocking God. Totally insensitive to Job's condition, Zophar denounced Job for being stubborn and unheeding of their advice to repent. Since God wasn't on the stage in person, Zophar considered himself a worthy substitute and able to tell Job exactly what the Almighty would say. And what the Almighty would say, Zophar hissed, was that Job was a despicable, sinning wretch. Otherwise, why would Job be having such a hard time? Big sins mean big troubles, Zophar scolded, and big troubles mean big sins.

Job interrupted. He was fed up with his friends' tedious moralizing. "Wisdom will die with you," Job sighed sarcastically (12:2). Repudiated and alone, he had not been given any help. No one understood; no one had any clues. In his misery, Job questioned why the evil people apparently thrive. "The tents of robbers are at peace," he reminded his friends, "and those who provoke God are secure . . ." (12:6). Job angrily told them that he had never robbed, never provoked God, yet look how he suffered. *Why?* Defiantly, Job screamed "Not guilty!" seventeen times. Why wouldn't God and why wouldn't his friends recognize that he was a man of integrity? Why did they persist in denouncing him as such a sinner?

Emotionally, Job stated that he wanted to have it out with God. He wanted God to cross-examine him, announcing defiantly that he was prepared to answer any question God might have. Why wouldn't God listen? Why was God absent to those who needed Him? Job sobbed a kind of nonprayer to the silent God, "Why dost thou hide thy face, and count me as thy enemy?" (13:24).

The man who felt abandoned by everyone, including God, lamented that even a tree when it is blown over will send up fresh, green shoots on the shattered stump, whereas Job was utterly without a future. Why, Job mused, couldn't a man have at least as much hope as a tree has? Why couldn't God put him in the deep freeze of death for the time being, then recall him when God's unexplained anger had passed?

Job caught himself talking about the nonexistence of the grave, and found himself suddenly besieged with new questions. "If a man die, shall he live again?" (14:14).

Through all of his tirades and doubts and queries about God, however, Job could not really bring himself to believe that God would not ultimately remember him. Job whispered, ". . . I would wait, till my release should come. Thou wouldest call, and I would answer thee . . ." (14:15).

With long, dull, repetitious speeches, Job's callers continued to barrage him with theological reasons for his condition. They solemnly mouthed shallow platitudes as if they were Holy Writ. They dumped pulpitsful of maxims similar to CRIME DOES NOT PAY, A CLEAR CONSCIENCE MEANS A PROSPEROUS LIFE, SUFFERING DEVELOPES CHARACTER. Bildad even attacked where it really hurt Job by telling Job that the root cause of his woes was undoubtedly his children's sins. To a man whose heart had already been broken by the loss of his children, Bildad's remarks pulverized Job's feelings. Eliphaz, Bildad, and Zophar proved not to be comforters but accusers. In the name of their rigid little dogmas, they guarded their religious tradition but imprisoned genuine faith.

After their second round of sermons, Job lost patience completely with them. Their glib answers were nothing but hot air. Job told them that it was easy to talk when they were not hurting. Advice comes cheap when one has no pain. They didn't understand what it was like when God decided to hold target practice and you were the target. "He has set me up as His target," Job told them, to their consternation. (*See* chapter 19.)

Job, broken by suffering and almost incapable of coherent thought, despaired so deeply that he could only mumble that "God has put me in the wrong, and closed his net about me" (19:6). Job realized that there was no possibility of getting his case settled with God during his life.

What about after he died, Job wondered. Was there any point of contact with God after death? A man who is dead can do nothing for himself, but Job felt that *someone* must care for his interests. Would there be any champion?

With absolutely no evidence whatsoever, Job affirmed that he was certain that eventually he would stand in the presence of that Someone, face-to-face. He dared to say that he was confident that he would be vindicated by the Supreme Judge of the universe! Although his physical frame would soon disintegrate completely, Job was certain that death would not cut him off from the Creator. "I know that my Redeemer lives . . ." Job suddenly announced, "and after my skin has been thus destroyed, then without my flesh I shall see God . . ." (19:25, 26).

Job knew intuitively, on a visceral level, that someday, some-how, some way, that the Great Someone would redress his grievances.

Job had resolved his own questions about God's silence by progressing to a sort of love-hate intimacy with the Hidden One.

Job, however, still wanted his questions answered. "Why do the wicked live, reach old age, and grow mighty in power?" (21:7). Job was hurt, confused, and angered at his friends' asser-tions that piety pays off and suffering is a sign of sin. Job pointed to notoriously evil neighbors in the community who prospered, watched their children grow up safely, sang and danced through life, ended their days in happiness, and died in peace. Job reminded his listeners that these characters not only ig-nored their responsibilities and had an easy time of it, but even mocked God. What was the point of being good, Job sourly complained.

The theological threesome shrilly reopened its seminar. Eli-phaz, Bildad, and Zophar vied with each other to set Job straight. Like most "God talk" by humans, it was partly right and partly wrong, a blend of fanaticism and foolishness. They correctly stressed the need for man's respect stretching up to-ward God, but they incorrectly omitted the news of God's *agape* care streaming down toward men. Job's friends properly emphasized God's sovereignty, but overlooked Job's suffering. They displayed creedal orthodoxy but were devoid of humanity. Full of words but empty of love, they had kept their religion in their heads without allowing it to spread to their hearts or their hands.

The arguments returned repeatedly to three dreary topics: God punishes us to get even; God deliberately tests us; God can do as He pleases to keep us in our place.

Job questioned their theses. (Is God a petty-minded account-ant, who remembers every slight and injury, who arranges to settle His grudges by inflicting insidiously cruel forms of heart-ache? Does God test us? Is He a brutal coach who intends to toughen us up so we can "take it?" Is this universe, as George Bernard Shaw once sarcastically wrote, "a moral gymnasium built expressly to strengthen your character in"? Does God, the unmoved, unmovable Mover, plot pain to tell us that we are weak and useless compared to Him? Does He, in His impassive and detached aloofness, arrange for us to suffer just to remind us that He can do as He pleases?)

Job's hunch was that if any of these questions could be answered with a yes it meant that God actually did not care about Job. Job finally shut off the infuriating sermonizing of Eliphaz, Bildad, and Zophar. He had more questions about God than before. All that his friends had done was to raise new doubt and uncertainty about God's ways.

Job's questions about God horrified his hearers. Job the heretic sounded like Job the blasphemer! Why was God so absent to those who needed Him? How could Job reach Him and present his cause? "Oh, that I knew where I might find Him . . ." Job grieved (23:3). Job indignantly demanded that God appear so that he could state his case to the Almighty Absentee. Face twitching with anger, Job snapped that if he could have a personal hearing with God, he might be able to pysch out the Lord's defenses, and perhaps take note of the Lord's reasoning. "I would learn what He would answer me. . . ." Job insisted (23:5), adding that God would finally see that He was contending with an honest man (*see* verse 7).

Why did God apparently refuse to discuss the matter, Job defiantly asked. Was there no justice ever? Why couldn't those who were oppressed by the wicked be given some explanation? "Why are not times of judgment kept by the Almighty . . ." Job thundered, "and why do those who know him never see his days?" (24:1).

To the God who had said *no* to Job's appeals for answers to his questions, Job poured out a bitter recitation of his innocence and frustration. Job punctuated every conversation with fresh challenges to God to speak up and give him some plausible explanation for the riddle of human misery. Why wouldn't God answer? Why did God remain deaf?

Finally, God answered Job. But not the way Job expected— or wanted. God let Job know that He, God, was still God. God made certain that Job understood that he was not God's equal, and that Job was still a human.

But God primarily let Job know that Job was not alone. God was there, too. God did not give answers to Job. He gave Job His Presence.

Job was content. God being what Job knew Him to be, Job could trust that God would arrange a solution for anything. Job, calm and satisfied with knowing God was present, spoke, "I had heard of thee by the hearing of the ear, but now my eye sees thee" (42:5). Job had moved from a hearsay understanding of a Great Someone to a personal awareness of the Presence.

Job's questions had not been answered by God. God said *no* to Job's demands for reasons. But Job didn't mind. Job's pain continued. The enigma of existence remained. But back of the enigma and in the midst of the pain, in the depths of his heart, Job sensed the evident presence and stunning might of the Lord. Job, the tortured questioner, could leave his unresolved doubts and unanswered problems, firmer in his faith than his narrowly orthodox friends.

Some bystanders watched a one-legged veteran painfully drag himself up the steps to a chapel. As the cripple clumsily worked himself toward the door, one onlooker cynically commented, "What's he expect—that God will grow him a new leg?"

Overhearing, the man without a leg turned and replied, "He always gives me enough to get along with the one I have."

Job learned this about God.

And so may we!

God has identified with us. He drew near, face-to-face, with all of us through that unique Personality of the Cross and the empty tomb. Through Jesus Christ, God does not give us answers to our jillion angry questions. He does not offer explanations. He does not deliver doctrines. He does not pose solutions. Instead, He gives us something better. He presents Himself!

It may well be that we will still have questions. But because of Jesus Christ, we will be able to put our questions in proper perspective. As Augustine, who himself painfully learned that faith must precede understanding, said, "Seek not to understand that thou mayest believe, but believe that thou mayest understand!"

Believing, we understand that God comes as Saviour, not as sadist. Suffering does not mean that He is angrily retaliating for insults and injuries. Rather than punish, He pities, "As a father pities his children, so the LORD pities those who fear him" (Psalms 103:13).

Job learned that God did not answer his demands for explanations. Job learned that God does not have to give an account of Himself to Job or anyone. More important, Job became conscious of God's presence with him in his hurts and loneliness.

We present-day Jobs also are promised God's sufficiency. We, too, discover that He gives more than answers to our whimpering "Why?" He shares His life with us. And, in turn, He means for us to represent His presence to each other and to those who are afflicted in any way.

A hopelessly ill woman, twisted and shriveled from years of suffering from deterioration of her spine, sentenced to a bed in an enormous ward of a state institution for incurables, sometimes had a visitor from her church. Other patients scoffed. "Hey, Myrtle, what's your church friend say to you that's so great?" a ward mate sneered one afternoon after the visitor left.

"Oh, nothing. Nothing at all, I guess," replied Myrtle from her bed; "she comes, and she just sits with me. But sometimes she cries with me."

We can give our presence. We can make incarnate now the concern which God has directed toward us. Without presuming to be God's proxy, we can provide God's kind of care.

8

Joseph, betrothed to Mary,
who decided to get a divorce

The man straightened up from his work and looked toward the West. It would soon be sunset, the start of the Sabbath. He felt a contented tiredness from long hours of sawing, drilling, and hammering each day during the six days from the last Sabbath, and he looked forward to the respite during the next twenty-four hours.

He gathered his carpenter's tools and carried them inside the tiny cottage. A desperately poor man, he looked after those tools with extreme care. He was still paying the money lender for the loan to buy the costly chisel and saw. As he wiped each tool and laid it gently in the box, the carpenter remembered the investment each article represented. He also remembered with some pride, however, that he knew how to work with that chisel and saw. It gave him a sense of standing and accomplishment to realize that he was slowly getting a reputation as a competent craftsman. Those tools, he reflected, would also be passed on to his yet-unborn sons. What better inheritance than the equipment to make a decent living?

As he considered those sons-to-be who would ultimately fall heir to those carpenter's tools, the man also thought of his betrothed. How extraordinarily fortunate he was, he thought, to be bound to such a girl as his Mary. A good wife, he recalled the rabbi's teaching, was the chief delight a man could hope for.

The carpenter glanced around the small, one-room building to which he would soon bring his Mary. He had built the cottage himself, and partitioned off the one room into two sections, half for the humans and half for the animals, as with most Nazareth dwellings. The low, square hut (not far removed from cave-dweller style by our standards) looked the same as the other peasant hovels straggling among the olive trees in the Galilean hill country, but the carpenter knew that Mary looked forward to the time when she would move to it as his wife.

"Be fruitful and multiply . . ." the verse in Genesis (1:22) read, and because it is the first law in the Torah, it held an important place for pious Jews, as well as being part of statutory law in Judaism. The betrothed carpenter pondered the economic benefits of producing a family.

The Jewish Talmud says that in the world to come, the first three questions asked of a man are, "Did you buy and sell in good faith? Did you have a set time for study? Did you raise a family?" Marrying his betrothed, Mary, and raising a family to the devout carpenter were more than ways of offsetting loneliness and helping the finances; marriage and children were solemn religious obligations.

The carpenter took his religion seriously. Not only did he buy and sell in good faith, never overcharging or performing shoddy work; he also spent some time each week in the Nazareth synagogue.

After he finished washing, he reentered the hut and changed into his only other garment—his "sabbath robe." He picked up his *tallith*, or prayer shawl, and walked down the path to the village synagogue. The carpenter reverently recited the ancient Hebrew prayers, and chanted the responses.

After the sundown prayers sounded the eerie, insistent blast of the *shofar*, the ram's horn, trumpeting the beginning of another Sabbath for Nazareth. The happy, contented sounds of children laughing, as families gathered for Sabbeth meals, sounded from every tiny hovel. Soon, the man reflected, his Mary and he would live together as man and wife, celebrating Sabbaths as joyously as anyone ever did in Nazareth. This Sabbath night, however, he would eat with his beloved Mary at her home.

"Joseph," she spoke, after she gave him the customary Sabbath peace greeting. Her voice always conveyed a shyness and yet a warmth to her man.

Joseph, the carpenter, gravely returned her greeting, but smiled tenderly at her. He followed her into the small area outside her family cottage where most meals were eaten. It was comfortably shaded by a couple of olive trees and a grape arbor. The rest of the family offered Sabbath blessings on Joseph and Joseph responded.

The meal was plain, peasant fare, but the freshly baked, flat barley loaves and tasty vegetable stew prepared by Mary made Joseph's mouth water. Joseph quietly watched as the family went through the ancient but meaningful Sabbath rituals of lighting the tiny Sabbath lamp, singing the haunting melodies of the blessings, sharing the cup of wine. He caught Mary's eye at one point, and wondered if she was thinking, as he was, of the times when they soon would usher in the happy Sabbath with such celebration in their own home. As the meal progressed from main course to fruits and another final bowl of wine, Joseph noticed that Mary looked particularly radiant and yet at the same time seemed somewhat distant. He longed to touch her, to hold her tight in his arms. The fleeting wish that this were their wedding night flashed through his mind.

Anxious though Joseph was to take Mary home with him, the pious carpenter scrupulously honored all the Jewish engagement, betrothal, and marriage customs. It was completely unthinkable to Joseph to do otherwise.

Among us, both civil law and canon law state that only the ceremony of marriage is binding and absolute. An engagement, while an agreement, is not an irrevocable contract to us, and a broken engagement is not considered damaging unless there are scandalous circumstances.

In New Testament times, the Jews had two steps preceding marriage, instead of our one. The second step was called betrothal, but established a permanent contract between the man and woman which is not inherent in our betrothal custom. Betrothal was considered almost as irrevocable as marriage. In the case of a girl being married for the first time, she was placed under the jurisdiction of her betrothed for a period of one year.

Although the affianced couple did not live together, betrothal conferred most of the privileges of marriage. The future husband could legally take possession of his betrothed during that year while she was still living at her parent's house and if she became pregnant, the child born under those circumstances would be considered legitimate. Usually, however, the girl remained a virgin throughout the betrothal period until she was married.

It was assumed that both the man and the woman would be faithful to one another during the year of betrothal. Infidelity during this premarriage time of betrothal ranked with adultery. The law—see Deuteronomy 22:23, 24—laid down a strict penalty for those guilty of adultery in the Jewish community: death by stoning. The same harsh measure could be used by a betrothed husband against his fiancée, if she were caught cheating on him during the betrothal.

Joseph had committed himself to Mary. To him, the commitment was permanent. He had covenanted with her to be faithful and caring for as long as either still was alive. Although the contract had not been formally completed by the actual marriage ceremony or yet consummated by the sex act, Joseph knew that he was legally and morally bound to Mary for good. The devout Nazareth carpenter had given his word to Mary that he would be a responsible and caring husband. And Joseph had no intention of going back on his word—ever. He was betrothed to Mary, and Joseph meant that relationship to be as strong and indissoluble as the joints of the cabinetwork he fashioned in his carpenter shop.

The custom of betrothal seldom bothered Joseph. He knew that the arrangement meant that no other man could press his attentions on Mary. Also, it set Mary aside as Joseph's woman while he got on his feet financially.

Much as he longed to have Mary live with him during their betrothal, Joseph refused to compromise his loyalty to the law or to ask Mary to give in to his lust. They made plans for the time when they would share the same bed and house, but they did not sleep together.

The night of their Sabbath meal together, Joseph felt a vague sense of uneasiness after saying good-night to Mary. The carpenter, used to the solid feel of tools and wood, did not rely much on intuition. Joseph felt uncomfortable when his subjective reactions intruded. Nonetheless, he was disquieted by his fiancée's manner and expression during the evening. There seemed to be nothing which Joseph could identify as specific evidence, but still something seemed to have been bothering Mary. He cared very deeply about her, and he did not like thinking that something troubled her. It particularly disturbed Joseph to think that if something were on Mary's mind, she apparently could not bring herself to disclose it to her betrothed.

The following day during the Sabbath, he walked to Mary's house—it was less than the permitted Sabbath-day's journey. To Joseph's consternation, she still seemed remote. When he asked her if something was on her mind, she answered hastily that everything was all right. Joseph detected, however, that she seemed to withdraw more after his question. The rest of the visit seemed awkward. When he prepared to leave, he thought that Mary appeared particularly anxious. He paused and waited for her to say something, but she merely bade him the usual tender *Shalom*. To Joseph, it looked as if she were about to cry when he walked away.

The news of Mary's departure the following day traveled via the gossip telegraph to every house in Nazareth by afternoon. One or two of the women filling their water jars at the town spring early in the morning had noticed Mary hurrying down the path out of town and had commented on this unusual event to the other housewives. Why was she leaving? Why the rush? Why was she alone? Did Joseph know? Where would she go? When would she return? To villagers forced to live most of their days in ho-hum humdrum, Mary's unexplained dawn departure offered a welcome relief from monotonous conversations about families, weather, crops, livestock, taxes, and petty domestic crises—dull subjects, and topics which long ago had been milked dry of all conversational value since everyone in Nazareth already knew what every other villager thought about all of these relatively trivial matters. But Mary's leaving the village so early in the morning without any apparent reason? This was a rich, brothy item to discuss at the well, on the paths, in the courtyards, and shops.

When Nazareth learned that neither Joseph nor Mary's family could provide a satisfactory reason for Mary's hasty exit, the topic immediately moved to top position of interest. For once, even such favorite conversation pieces as Roman oppression and Galilean guerrillas were eclipsed. Nazareth sought explanations for Mary's bizarre departure. Within the day, several "knowing" persons stated what most secretly suspected; namely, that Mary was pregnant.

Galilean villages, like small towns throughout the world, had their own tough codes and controls. If a girl flouted them, she was as good as dead. Especially in the realm of sex, a girl who was even suspected of violating the taboos was ostracized as a whore. The area had its share of stories, each sad and sordid, which were whispered confidentially.

Joseph was incoherent with shock and grief when he heard that Mary had left town. Instinctively, he rushed to her house. He queried Mary's family, but, like everyone else in Nazareth, he could find no clues from the menfolk. Joseph suspected that Mary's mother might be able to offer some ideas, but he found her tearful and uncommunicative.

Joseph, drained of purpose, slowly trudged back to his carpenter shop. Mechanically, he picked up a saw. That day, he worked far past his usual quitting time. It was dark when he finally put down his tools, wearily washed his hands, and munched a few mouthfuls of bread. Too exhausted to think, he stumbled to his sleeping mat.

Like a man grievously wounded, the carpenter shuffled silently to customers, transacted his business with them with a minimum of small talk, then walked away from them to resume his work. It seemed too painful to Joseph to talk about anything. Most of all, of course, he wanted to avoid discussing the subject of Mary.

No one had to tell Joseph what most of Nazareth thought. Joseph had heard the raucous laughter in the donkey market where the male members of the village and surrounding area met regularly to haggle over livestock and exchange anecdotes. Joseph had previously heard the many off-color stories of how hot-blooded Iberian troopers came down from the garrisons with enough silks and sweet talk to lure local lasses into a walk in the hills. Joseph knew that the boys were making cracks about his Mary and an alleged legionnaire lover.

As the days of Mary's absence glided into weeks, Nazareth tired of squeezing scandal out of her departure and life settled down to its usual dull dogtrot for everyone except Joseph. Joseph stolidly continued to try to cope with the hurt and loneliness of Mary's leaving. He prayed. He worked. He attended the Torah reading at synagogue. He ate. He slept. Although many in the village sensed that he was aching, Joseph could not share the pain with anyone.

Mary returned as suddenly as she had departed. She had been gone for over three months, and some of the more suspicious villagers immediately did quick arithmetic to determine whether or not a full-term pregnancy could have occurred, and not able to reach a clear-cut conclusion, studied Mary's profile for signs that she was carrying a baby. At least, as some of the busy tongues observed, she didn't come traipsing home with a child. The fact that Mary came home allayed the dark doubt and the nasty gossip which had been passed around at the time of her departure. Peasant girls who got into trouble with a man inevitably stayed away for good.

Joseph had ambivalent feelings when he heard that Mary had returned to her home in Nazareth. On one hand, he wanted to rush joyously to her side. At the same time, he felt an icy fear that she would have changed. All the nagging, unanswered questions which had been left dangling for three months came to his mind. Why had she left? Why hadn't she told him? Was something wrong?

Joseph cleaned up and walked gravely to Mary's father's house. He stiffly acknowledged the family, and greeted his long-absent fiancée. Words came clumsily to the carpenter. He listened to Mary's halting explanation of her whereabouts during the preceding months—a long trip south to the Judean hill country and a lengthy visit with her cousin, Elizabeth, and her husband, Zechariah. Joseph could tell that Mary was telling the truth to him, but he could not attach adequate reasons for such an absence. Later, after the meal when they walked out under the trees by themselves, Joseph heard Mary's report of Elizabeth's baby—an astonishing story because of Elizabeth's advanced years. Joseph, bewildered at Mary's tale of God intervening to enable her cousin to have a child, thought that he detected that Mary was trying to tell him something. The report seemed complicated and full of additional unspoken agenda, and Joseph wished that everything were as plain and obvious as the lines on his measuring stick and lumber. He prepared to walk her back to her parents' cottage.

She caught his sleeve and made him stop. There was something else which she had to tell him.

Joseph's head reeled when he heard her announcement. He could hardly sort out her words after he heard the first part about her going to have a baby. Dimly, later, he recalled her trying to tell him about God sending a messenger, and that she had never consorted with any other man. All that Joseph really heard were the dread words that Mary was pregnant.

Grim-faced, the carpenter abruptly turned and stalked away. He returned to his own hut and collapsed with a low moan to his mat. He felt tears welling in his eyes and he began to sob uncontrollably. Later, he regained his composure and tried to make plans for the future.

Momentarily, Joseph had the impulsive desire to see justice done to the fullest. He knew that his case was airtight, and that he could stand on his rights and have Mary stoned to death for infidelity. After all, it was in the law, he reminded himself. Besides, Joseph angrily argued to himself, such a stern application of the law just might warn other girls not to trifle with God's commandments.

Basically a just man, Joseph quickly overcame his fleeting thoughts for revenge and punishment. His most decent course of action, he made up his mind, would be a quiet divorce. The betrothal would be terminated with a minimum of fuss and adverse publicity for Mary.

Joseph began to phrase the wording of the bill of divorcement which he would have to have drawn up. He intended to treat Mary with as much consideration as he could but scratched his head in puzzlement. How could he be delicate in describing his reasons for divorcing her? After all, adultery meant that the tie between them had been severed in the most insensitive way. He winced as he reflected that Mary had apparently consented to lie with a Roman soldier or some other man after pledging herself to Joseph. The carpenter choked back the wave of hurt and anger that threatened to engulf him when he thought of Mary's infidelity. He prostrated himself on his sleeping mat and prayed—and prayed.

He fell off to sleep, and woke some hours later in the middle of the night with the conviction that God had let it be known that divorce was out of the question. How could this be? Joseph wondered. Was not his betrothed pregnant—and obviously not by Joseph? Surely, Joseph reasoned, he was doing the most humane thing under the circumstances. Divorce was the just way, the way to save Mary as much shame as possible.

God said *no* to Joseph, who planned to divorce Mary. Instead, God commanded the Nazareth carpenter to accept Mary, unborn child and all, as his wife.

Joseph, with no evidence except Mary's word that she had not slept with another man and no proof except God's promise that Mary's story was not a lie, kept his commitment to Mary. Joseph understood that God had made a commitment to the human community to be a loving and faithful God. In response, Joseph knew that his relationship with Mary was the same kind of commitment to be loving and faithful—as long as either was still alive.

According to the *New York Times* (March 3, 1973), in 1972 the number of marriages in the United States rose slightly to 2,-269,000. But the number of divorces and annulments rose even more rapidly to 839,000. Statistically, therefore, more than one-third as many marriages broke up legally last year as were entered into. And the number of divorces was more than 80 percent higher than ten years ago. Obviously, marriage as a form of lifetime commitment between a husband and wife is changing fast.

In New York, at a recent symposium on new patterns of marriage between a man and a woman, some participants expressed interest in the "revolving-door concept," where a person may go from lover to lover—even while in a marriage relationship—and extolled "freedom to exit" as a great new marriage idea. "The free marriage," as labeled by one panelist, with no demands of responsibility or commitment, allegedly permits both partners to "fulfill themselves," to "find their identities," to "liberate themselves from restrictive life situations."

The God who has committed Himself to us insists on a likeminded commitment on the part of each marriage partner. In fact, the symbolism and terminology used in the Bible for the relationship of God to us and the relationship of us to each other in marriage is exactly the same. Every relationship between God and us is based on covenant—the agreement or pact in which God promises that He will ever be faithful to us. And every enduring relationship between marriage partners is also based on covenant—the pact in which each promises fidelity to the other. A covenant in the Bible meant both Israel's exclusive devotion to the one God, and a man's or woman's exclusive devotion to his or her spouse.

This kind of commitment is for keeps. It is totally removed from the superficial vow taken by one movie starlet in which she and her husband inserted the words in their marriage promise, ". . . as long as we both shall be happy."

Throwaway partners are nothing new. Joseph was tempted to discard Mary. Every husband and every wife in history could find some excuse for divorce. And every married person secretly knows that marriage demands commitment, responsibility, fidelity—and a lot of other words which today may sound faintly quaint, a bit square, a little old-fashioned, and perhaps even somewhat unreal in an age of playboys and libbers.

The covenanting God has given His word to us that He will not desert us. That promise has been sealed in blood—literally!

Before we can comprehend what it means to be lovers, we must first understand that the Lover, the One whose care created us and keeps us, is the model and motivator for meaningful relationships. Indeed, apart from the One who insisted on being pinned down to the point of dying for us, our marriages decline into alliances—empty, fleeting, and demeaning. Permanent commitment to one's marriage partner turns out to be realistic.

As Joseph—undergirded by God's Promise—firmly determined to reject divorce, he learned that in the Lord's arithmetic, forgetting the *I* to become a *we* is a one plus one equaling three: a husband, a wife, and the Presence of the covenanting God!

9

Jesus,
who prayed to escape suffering

Gethsemane. The word means "oil press." It was a significant name for the place where Jesus felt ground and crushed by the events of His final hours on earth. Squeezed, pressed, and pulverized like a ripe olive caught under the enormous revolving stone, mashing the once-luscious piece of fruit to a tiny shred of worthless pulp, Jesus' life was about to be quashed. The wheel of humiliation, defeat, and death would quickly grind Him into nothingness. *Gethsemane,* for Jesus, meant not only the Place of the Oil Press but the place of His greatest personal duress.

"My sorrow is crushing the life out of me," is a possible translation of Jesus' words recorded in Mark 14:34. All of the Gospel writers recording the episode in the Place of the Oil Press emphasized that Jesus' words indicated that the anguish that night was overwhelming. Luke described it with the Greek word *agonia,* meaning an agonizingly anxious experience—a crunching contest in which a victim is almost overcome.

Luke, with his physician's attention to detail, recorded some of the medical aspects of that experience for Jesus. Luke noted that Jesus' "sweat became like great drops of blood . . ." (22:44). Medical dictionaries describe this condition as *chromhaidrosis,* and state that intense emotional stress may cause secretion of colored perspiration. There are numerous case histories of chromhaidrosis. For example, DeMezeray records that Charles IX of France, during the last two weeks of his life in May 1574, was so affected by strain that "his condition made strange efforts

97

... blood gushed from all the outlets of his body, even from the pores of his skin so that on one occasion he was found bathed in a bloody sweat."

Our salvation really took place at Gethsemane. The great wringing and crushing of Jesus which was concluded on the cross was decided on the Place of the Oil Press. Gethsemane, for Jesus, was the Calvary of His soul. Golgotha was the Calvary of His body. The crucifixion of Jesus' spirit occurred in the Garden of the Oil Press. The Crucifixion of His flesh took place on the beam on the stake at the Place of the Skull.

Emotional torment is always more intolerable than physical torture. The wracking of Jesus' mind and spirit was worse than the racking of His limbs and torso.

Gethsemane: The Place of the Press. For Jesus, the experience crunched Him with such mental anguish and emotional strain that He pleaded for release. Gethsemane stands for Jesus' struggle for sanity. At the Place of the Oil Press, Jesus found Himself crushed in unbearable conflict between human desire and the divine will. The veil of the mystery of two natures of the One whom we acclaim as the God-Man was momentarily lifted, and Jesus the human struggled to obey the will of the Father.

Some disparage Jesus' suffering in Gethsemane as a sign of weakness. Some point to other martyrs, stating that they died without the intense emotional agony which Jesus displayed.

"Look at Socrates," one critic of the faith informed a collegiate audience. "Socrates didn't anguish over his impending death. He stoically took the hemlock. He proudly held his head high to the end."

True, Socrates preserved his remarkable dignity throughout. He also retained his pose of self-righteousness and tried to vindicate himself. Socrates cheerfully defended himself and refused to forsake his principles. He was willing to accept the death penalty to remain true to his convictions. At the end, the great teacher-philosopher calmly accepted the fatal cup. Socrates died for himself.

Jesus had to die for others.

Those "others," however, posed special problems. It is one

thing to be asked to lay down life for one's own principles and convictions. It is another to be asked to die with and for certain worthy individuals. It is an entirely different matter to volunteer to identify with the most despicable segment of society— even to the point of enduring a disgraceful execution for them.

A cross has been so sentimentalized by so many generations of songwriters and preachers that it no longer has any sting. A cross is now merely a decorative trinket around one's neck or on an altar. A vague symbol for religion, a cross has become so innocuous and inoffensive to moderns that spring-flower shows feature it as part of the floral layout and downtown buildings at Easter time nightly outline a cross in lighted skyscraper windows. Few remember today that a cross originally was the instrument of torturous death reserved for the most loathsome and depraved criminals.

In our culture, if we were to reserve a cross for certain offenders, we would inflict a cross only on dope pushers and evil-minded degenerates who recruit children into prostitution or other forms of perversion. We would reserve a cross for hate-filled cultists who kill for kicks, for cunning sadists who kidnap and torture, for treacherous traitors who sell out the nation or plot anarchy. To gain some notion of how scandalously inglorious a cross was to Jesus' generation, think of the most detestable and offensive human you can imagine who, in your opinion, might deserve the death penalty. This is the kind of person who would have been among "the others" for whom Jesus was asked to die!

Part of the anguish of the night at the Place of the Oil Press came when Jesus had to face up to dying for these kinds of "others." "Must I submit to the same humiliation as these?" Jesus, in effect, asked. "Must I bear the same stigma, the same sentence, the loathing, as criminals and turncoats? Must I stand with these? Do I have to be cursed and hated as one who goes to a cross? Is there any way to vindicate myself?"

Furthermore, Jesus recognized the ghastly finality and utter nothingness of death. "Must I submit to the total oblivion of the Valley of the Shadow?" He demanded.

Mature people may be able to bring themselves to cope with

dying. Dying, the physical act of surrendering all physiological processes, can be compared to going to sleep. Dying is like the lights all going out, whether winking off one at a time, or all blacking out at once through massive power failure. Although mature persons may learn to face the experience of dying, no one can willingly accept death. Dying and death are two separate problems. Death means extinction. Death means nonbeing, nonexistence, noneverything.

Jesus was no Hindu holy man, renouncing the earth and all material things. Nor was Jesus a Buddhist priest, trying to escape all sensation and desire. Rather, Jesus had a wholesome Jewish enjoyment for life. He relished His associations with others. He had a healthy zest for a tasty meal.

Jesus was no morose neurotic with death wishes. He did not welcome His demise anymore than anyone would who is of sound mind and body. He was only thirty, and life is sweet for any healthy, young human. He appreciated everything about life on this earth, and knew that it was good. As the astronauts who returned after viewing the planet from the moon, or POWs who suffered deprivation, or patients snatched from the morgue by medical miracles all testify, this world is immensely pleasant and beautiful. Jesus, who had watched the sun set over water and heard the laughter of little children, who had tasted the savory lamb roast at Passover, and touched the grass, soft and cool with early-morning dew, shrank from the yawning nothingness of the Pit. Death, to Jesus, was the Enemy.

Was there no way out? He wondered that night in the Place of the Oil Press. Could He not escape the horrors of death—at least for the present?

Did the thought cross His mind of vaulting the wall, sneaking through back paths and avoiding patrols, hiking north for six or seven hours until daylight, then holing up in a cave during the daylight hours? After all, He *could* have escaped. He *could* have jumped out of the danger zone of Jerusalem and fled to safety. He *could* have retired to obscurity in Galilee, kept out of the headlines, survived to a ripe old age, and died in bed.

Moreover, Jesus asked, did He have to submit to defeat?

"Must I permit evil to overwhelm me?" He in effect prayed.

The stone wheel of hellish forces was oil pressing Him. Diabolic powers were pulverizing Him. Everything good was being ground to pulp. Was there no way of showing His superiority? Was there no way for Jesus to seize victory for Himself and His cause without enduring such hopeless suppression?

His cause? Look at it—lying over there under the tree, in the form of a few snoring lumps. These heavy-lidded dullards who had said they would go to any lengths for God's rule but who were so unreliable they couldn't even sit up with Him for a while—*they* were instruments of Jesus' cause.

These shaky supporters were no bulwark against the satanic might which was moving to defeat Jesus. Jesus knew that one of these supporters had already defected. Indeed, Jesus suspected, this deserter, Judas Iscariot, was undoubtedly on his way with a posse to grab Jesus and march Him off to the grand finale of the debacle: Crucifixion.

His own people, the eminent and law-abiding leaders of the temple, the respectable, dues-paying, card-carrying Pharisees, the superreligious scribes who poured over the sacred texts, had rejected Him. Scorned and repudiated by everyone who should have welcomed Him or taken Him seriously, Jesus knew that He had been deserted.

In His isolation, He wondered if there were not some way of reversing the tide of evil forces. Could He not overwhelm the combined powers of His countrymen's greed, pride, and hate which were about to destroy Him?

Jesus prayed. "My Father," He began, using the first person singular *my*—the only time Jesus ever addressed the Father in this way *(see* Matthew 26:39,42). ". . . all things are possible to thee. . . ." Jesus continued (Mark 14:36), underscoring Jesus' certainty that God, if He chooses, can provide an alternative to the cross.

". . . remove this cup from me . . ." Jesus pleaded in the same verse. He begged God to excuse Him from having to drain the cup of suffering. Was there no other way of accomplishing the Father's will without that cup? Was there any possibility of another means of obedience?

It was the prayer of a desperate man. Both Mark and Luke

use a verb form in Greek to show that Jesus prayed to be relieved of His cup of suffering not once but over and over. Luke's account shows broken phrases, reflecting the panting plea and desperate gasps of a man so distraught that He could not arrange His words in complete sentences. Matthew and Mark recall that Jesus three times implored the Father to remove the cup. Jesus begged and pleaded repeatedly for a way out, returning several times to rouse the sleepy-eyed followers who kept dozing off.

"Do I have to walk this lonesome valley?" Jesus cried. "Is there no way out?" Could there be no messiahship without a cross? Was there no way of obedience without suffering for others? Could He not complete His mission without pain and disgrace? Was there no easier way? no secure, successful way?

"Remove this cup," bared this humanness of the Mediator. He struggled to impose His own will.

Even Jesus' prayer was not answered the way in which He asked. In a sense, the Father said *no* to the Son at Gethsemane. God, however, did answer.

Jesus finally prayed, ". . . nevertheless not my will, but thine, be done" (Luke 22:42). He knew that He would be strengthened to walk the lonesome valley. He adjusted His will to the will of the Father. Jesus acquiesced in the plan of the Eternal One. He chose to accept His mission of suffering.

"Not my will, but thine, be done," is not a resigned sigh, in which Jesus glumly gave in to fate or some impersonal *kismet.* "Thy will be done," is not the weary surrender of a trapped, doomed man who despondently accepts the inevitable. "Father, Thy will be done!" is a shout of trust!

The Father's plan, God's rule, the Almighty's work will be carried out, Jesus affirmed. And in His case, Jesus acknowledged that this entailed total and absolute surrender to the needs of others. Furthermore, Jesus accepted that His surrender to the needs of others meant laying down His life as a crucified criminal. While the cross would apparently terminate Jesus' work, Jesus trusted that in actuality the cross would germinate His work!

Jesus did not merely talk about God's rule and God's will. He lived it. And He died it.

Christ did not agonize in the Place of the Oil Press to give you "a religious mood." His sacrifice demands your sacrifice.

You have been given the gift of living and dying just one death. You may live and die that one death either by crucifixion or by suicide. These are ultimately the only two ways.

You may die for others, or you may perish in self. You may grow conscious of the gift of life, or you may become obsessed with the absurdity of existence. You may lay down your energies, your time, and your goods for others, or you may stockpile self until it crushes you.

Choose, then, to take up your life and death—and commit crucifixion!

An accountant recently had a client demand that the accountant approve certain questionable tax deductions. The accountant refused. The client took his business elsewhere. Losing a good-paying client, the accountant raised the oil-press prayer, "Is there any way out? Let this cup pass from me!"

A supervisor tried to help a man in his department who had serious family and personal problems. The supervisor knew that the most expedient thing would have been to fire the employee, but he knew that the employee would have difficulty in finding another job in his present condition. Later, after everything had straightened out satisfactorily, the supervisor learned that he was to be passed over for a promotion. Rumor had it that the reason was that the supervisor was too softhearted. The supervisor, enduring his private Gethsemane, pleaded for a way out, for the cup to be removed.

A father denied himself all luxuries and practiced severe economics to finance his son's college education. In the middle of the son's final year, after enduring great personal sacrifice for nearly four years, the father received a note from his son stating that he had dropped out of school. The parent anguished for some way out, for his personal cup of suffering to be removed.

A housewife, recalling the once-promising career as a buyer she had left ten years ago, remembered that she had enjoyed financial independence, daily challenges, and the esteem of business-world colleagues. Today, she notices her wrinkles, nurses three children with colds, cooks for a taciturn husband, and endures a boring round of being chauffeur, maid, and wash-woman. Must she make all this sacrifice? Is there no way out? May her cup of suffering be removed?

To be hurt is to be alive. God experiences this through Jesus Christ. The alternative to being hurt and being alive is just a hollow, lonely existence that is worse than death.

Accountant, supervisor, parent, housewife, or whatever, you can take up your daily crosses for others with confidence. When you do agree to follow Him who shouldered the heaviest bur-den of history, you begin to pass from temptation to trust to triumph.

You will discover that when you walk your lonesome valley, you do not walk it alone. Someone, you learn, has already walked it before you—and for you. After the chill and dark of the shadow of anxiety, you are assured of the burst of warming, morning light at the end! Moreover, you discover the life-giving Lord joining you in your pilgrimage through the gardens and valleys.

10

James and John,
who asked for revenge

Such outrageous behavior screamed for a reprisal!

Hospitality was a basic duty. Turning away a guest—espe-cially a paying guest—was unthinkable. Entertaining a stranger in the village, in fact, was a sacred responsibility. Even an enemy received protection overnight. When some Samaritan villagers refused Jesus and His disciples food and a place to stretch out for the night, they were guilty of a serious breach of etiquette.

James and John, two of Jesus' associates, steamed with anger. The Samaritans' insult had stung and infuriated all the disciples, but James and John raged. Not for nothing had they been nick-named Sons of Thunder by Jesus.

The Samaritans again! Like all Galileans, James and John remembered an almost interminable list of rude and inhumane acts by Samaritans. Time does not necessarily heal all wounds; sometimes it merely covers them with scar tissue. James, John, and nearly all Jews had been slashed with too many insults and injuries from Samaritans to forget easily.

The two brothers remembered old Zebedee, their father, telling them stories of the atrocities committed by Samaritans through the centuries. James and John recalled the tales of treachery by Samaritans toward hapless Jews hobbling back to Jerusalem after years of exile in Babylon, some five hundred years earlier. James and John had heard of the countless mean ways the Samaritans had tried to impede the rebuilding of the

Jewish temple five centuries ago.

The Sons of Thunder had been taught the stories of the arrogant way the Samaritans had persisted in promoting their heretical cult. James and John, carefully nurtured in Judaism, had learned to resent the Samaritan claims. They knew that the Samaritan temple had been founded by a defrocked Jewish priest, and that the Samaritan sacred writings were selected pieces of Jewish sacred Scripture, pasted together cunningly to play up the Samaritan worship at Mount Gerizim. As James and John knew, the self-righteous Samaritans claimed that God ordained their Mount Gerizim to be the "navel of the universe," and identified their mountain as the site for nearly every holy event in history. James and John, growing up in Galilee, had heard the ridiculous claims about Mount Gerizim many times, how the Samaritans insisted that Mount Gerizim was where Adam was created out of dust, that Mount Gerizim was where Abel built the first altar, that Mount Gerizim was the only area not submerged by the Flood, that Mount Gerizim was where Noah sacrificed after the waters receded in the world, that Mount Gerizim was where Abraham prepared to sacrifice Isaac, that Mount Gerizim was where the twelve stones were erected after the Israelites entered the Promised Land, that Mount Gerizim was where the Ark of the Covenant was hidden, that Mount Gerizim was where God insisted that all sacrifices be made and all true worship conducted. James and John felt the storm clouds of anger every time they thought of the insolent Samaritans and their fraudulent stories about their holy mountain.

The two sons of Zebedee had also been taught how despicably cowardly the Samaritans had been one hundred sixty years earlier when the brutal armies of Antiochus Epiphanes IV had overrun the Middle East. James's and John's ancestors had fought, bled, and died rather than submit to this tyrant and his atrocities. The Samaritans? James and John knew the dismal story of the Samaritan sellout. James and John had heard the tales of the way the Samaritan community took the easiest course in the face of Antiochus Epiphanes IV by toadying up to him, referring to him as a god, and asking to name the temple on Mount Gerizim after Jupiter, the chief deity in Greek mythology! Furthermore, as James and John hotly pointed out many times to strangers, the Samaritans stooped to selling untold numbers of Jews into slavery during the dark days of Antiochus Epiphanes IV before the Maccabean revolt rallied the Jewish community.

James and John knew for a fact that the Samaritans had not changed but continued to be just as churlish and cruel. Bitterly and angrily, they recalled the episode in Jerusalem about twenty years previously. James and John were only small boys in Galilee at the time, but they had heard so much about the incident then and later that they never forgot the details of how a group of Samaritans had sneaked into the Jewish temple in Jerusalem one night at Passover and desecrated the sacred place of worship by strewing human remains throughout the sanctuary. What, James and John demanded, could be more contemptible than defiling their place of worship during the height of the holy season?

This disgusting incident, James and John knew, had not been the last hostile act by the Samaritans. James and John had heard the eyewitness accounts of Samaritan raids on Jewish border villages. James and John had seen the charred ruins of Galilean houses, burned out by marauding Samaritan guerrillas. James and John had talked with Jewish farmers who had lost livestock or entire harvests to some of these rampaging Samaritans.

James and John had also talked with Jewish pilgrims who had been waylaid, beaten, and robbed while passing through Samaria. The shortest, easiest route between Galilee and Jerusalem lay through Samaria, and most Jews from the north going to or from the religious festivals at the Temple walked through Samaritan territory. James and John had heard dozens of cases of how hapless Jewish travelers were harassed or hurt by Samaritan bullies.

Nearly every month, when the signal fires were lighted to announce the start of the monthly religious celebrations so important to all Jews, some Samaritans would deliberately ignite beacons to mislead the faithful in Galilee. James and John had seen the flares set in Samaritan villages as a provocation against

Jewish worshipers. The Samaritans' false signals had inadvertently caused many of James's and John's devout friends to begin the new-month ceremonies too early, and James and John boiled with fury each time.

Inheriting a legacy of hate and suspicion toward everything Samaritan, James and John loathed their heretic neighbors. In fact, even the word "Samaritan" carried the force of a vulgar epithet. "Samaritan" was used to denounce (as the time when Jesus' critics spat, ". . . you are a Samaritan . . ." (John 8:48). Calling someone a Samaritan was the dirtiest name, the vilest term, and the grossest insult which James and John knew. Despising another as a Samaritan ranked with "cur" or "Gentile." James and John understood that respectable people avoided using such improper language altogether—as when the scribe, after hearing Jesus tell the Parable of the Good Samaritan and ask who was the neighbor to the man in need, priggishly refused to say the foul word "Samaritan" but answered Jesus' question with the words, "The one who showed mercy" (Luke 10:37). Roughhewn Galilean fishermen weren't as fastidious, and James and John occasionally let fly with "Samaritan!" at someone as a cussword.

On more polite occasions, when James and John and other Jews had to refer to Samaritans, they called them "Cuthians." "Cuthian" was not considered to be in such bad taste as "Samaritan," but it still conveyed the feelings of contempt all Jews felt toward all Samaritans since "Cuthian" meant an idolatrous foreigner (from 2 Kings 17:30 where "men of Cuth," one of the tribes deported from Persia and relocated near Shechem by the Assyrians, were believed—erroneously—to be the ancestors of the Samaritans).

Other times, James and John sneered at Samaritans by using the label "lion converts," referring to the time centuries earlier when Samaritan ancestors, superstitious and superficial, converted to Judaism out of terror because of some roving lions. Cuthians or Lion Converts, the nicknames for Samaritans, made no difference to the sons of Zebedee or to other Jews. James and John and all their countrymen dismissed Samaritans as degenerate, depraved, and despicable.

James and John, in fact, recognized that not only was inter-marriage with Samaritans prohibited by Jewish law, but that any contact with Samaritans was something which no Jew should stoop to. As schoolboys in the village synagogue, James and John had heard the rabbi's stern teachings about Samaritan perfidy:

> Two nations I detest,
> and a third is no nation at all:
> the inhabitants of Mount Seir, the Philistines,
> and the senseless folk that live at Shechem.

Ecclesiasticus 50:25,26 NEB

As boys James and John had repeated that Samaritans were "no nation at all" and "senseless folk." The young James and John had also heard that Samaritans "have no law nor even the remains of a law; therefore they are contemptible and corrupt" (Rabbi Simeon ben Johai). Samaritans, James and John had been instructed, were excluded from all Jewish ritual and cultic affairs. The two brothers had been informed as youths that in Jerusalem, there were laws against accepting a temple tax, a sin-offering or a guilt-offering from Samaritans.

Capping all this personal history of affronts and attacks by Samaritans on James and John was the evening when some Samaritan villagers rudely refused a simple request for food and shelter overnight. Such bad manners and lack of humanitarian concern infuriated the two brothers known for their violent tempers. The episode reinforced their feelings toward Samaritans.

It was time to teach these ingrates a lesson, James and John fumed. Give these Samaritans a dose of their own medicine! Punish them for such sullen insensitivity! James and John snorted that everyone had been mollycoddling the Samaritans for too long. A show of force, some stern reprisals—that's what the Samaritans would understand. Put them in their place once and for all! Let these dirty foreigners learn some lessons in good manners and basic hospitality! James and John assured each other that Jesus had been too soft toward Samaritans, too indulgent. The Samaritans needed to be reminded of how arrogant and cruel they had behaved. A bolt of lightning reducing those huts to charred rubble would be the best way of wising up the Samaritans! Enough of the sweet talk, James and John sputtered. Time to act—for a change!

Hadn't Jesus been telling His followers to be bold and resolute? Hadn't the rabbi solemnly urged them to take a stand when the time came? Very well, James and John told each other, they would take their stand. Here was the time and the place to draw the line against such obvious evil.

And hadn't Jesus promised His disciples power? Hadn't He bestowed authority on the Twelve? Here, against those Samaritan villagers, was the occasion to exercise their power and authority, James and John were convinced.

Not long before, James and John, along with Peter, had been given a vision of Elijah, the greatest Old Testament prophet. Elijah's story remained fresh in their minds. What, James and John asked themselves, had Elijah done when he had been faced with God's adversaries? Elijah had called down fire, hadn't he? Very well, James and John told each other, they would call down fire, too! What better precedent for raining destruction as punishment than Elijah? If it was all right with him, Israel's bravest spokesman for the Lord, James and John assured themselves, surely it also was all right for them.

Yes, the two angry disciples suggested to each other, God had approved hurling down fire in Elijah's day. In fact, they reminded themselves, the Lord was a wrathful God who sternly held all men and all nations accountable. James and John, saturated in the writings of their faith, recalled the dozens of biblical passages referring to God's judgment in terms of fiery punishment.

> For a fire is kindled by my anger,
>   and it burns to the depths of Sheol,
> devours the earth and its increase. . . .
>
>   (Deuteronomy 32:22)

For the Lord your God is a devouring fire, a jealous
God.

Deuteronomy 4:24

> who makest the winds thy messengers,
> fire and flame thy ministers.

Psalms 104:4

> For behold, the Lord will come in fire,
> and his chariots like the stormwind,
> to render his anger in fury,
> and his rebuke with flames of fire.

Isaiah 66:15

. . . in my anger a fire is kindled which shall burn for
ever.

Jeremiah 15:14

> . . . lest my wrath go forth like fire,
> and burn with none to quench it,
> because of your evil doings.

21:12

Therefore I have poured out my indignation upon
them; I have consumed them with the fire of my
wrath; their way have I requited upon their heads, says
the Lord God . . . I will send fire on Magog and on those
who dwell securely in the coastlands; and they shall
know that I am the Lord.

Ezekiel 22:31; 39:6

. . . Behold, the Lord God was calling for a judgment
by fire. . . .

Amos 7:4

For behold, the day comes, burning like an oven, when all the arrogant and evildoers will be stubble; the day that comes shall burn them up, says the Lord of hosts. . . .

Malachi 4:1

Armed with a powerful arsenal of proof texts, James and John strode toward Jesus. They were determined to act. A judgment on the wicked Samaritans! The day had come, the two brothers had decided, when all the arrogant and all the evildoers in that Samaritan village should be chastised with fiery punishment. Even the score with God's enemies! Pay back the insolent Cuthians!

Rubbing their hands with anticipation, the two self-appointed deputies for divine doom marched up to the Master to request permission to punish the Samaritan village. "Lord," they chorused, "do you want us to bid fire come down from heaven and consume them?" (Luke 9:54).

James and John, swelling with self-righteousness and honest indignation, waited for the signal to give the nod to God. They felt confident that Jesus would not let this offense go unnoticed. Furthermore, they sincerely believed that they were due a little respect and consideration. Hadn't they left their fishing boats to follow Jesus? Had not they endured the hardships, accepted the jibes, shared the dangers of being disciples of the most dynamic Israelite of all—the Jesus who they suspected was the long-awaited Messiah?

Jesus turned and looked His two fiery followers in the eye, first James, then John. For a long moment, He was silent. When He spoke, He said nothing—not a word—about the Samaritans. Instead, He rebuked James and John!

A curt *Permission denied!* is the divine answer to every request to wreak punishment on others. God barks a stern *no!* whenever He is asked to participate in schemes to bring retaliation on anyone.

Through Jesus, He rebuked James and John for descending to the same pit of revenge as the Samaritans. How could they be

instruments of peace, God's *shalom,* when they are itching to
retaliate? The sons of Zebedee should have known better. If
they could let a slight from a few insolent peasant villagers
upset them, what were these disciples going to do when they
came up against serious opposition?

Furthermore, who appointed James and John to mete out
punishments? This was God's prerogative, not theirs! Jesus put
James and John in their place—not the Samaritans.

We all secretly fancy ourselves uniquely endowed and divinely appointed to tell the Lord when to strike down wrongdo-
ers. Our speciality is the heavenly zap! Our favorite form of
service to God is advising Him when and how to punish others.

Judgment and punishment are God's business, however, not
ours. Settling the accounts with malefactors is the jealously
guarded responsibility of the Lord of all history. We have no
more right to assume judicial functions which properly belong
to the Almighty than we have to step in and take over for the
local police force.

"Vengeance is mine, I will repay, says the Lord" (Romans
12:19). We can leave the evildoer for God to deal with. He has
the last word with everyone, even with Samaritan villagers. It
is no concern of ours to see to it that someone else gets what's
coming to him. God arranges that. And He insists on reserving
those arrangements for Himself.

Life for most of us slips down into a grudge match. Part of the
weariness which we all feel comes from conducting the many
personal vendettas against those who have hurt us. Even
though many of these vendettas may be secret and carried out
only in our thoughts, they still take immense time and thought
and energy, and they still leave us tired from fighting. We are
obsessed with redressing slights to our personal honor. We insist
on avenging swipes against our dignity.

Like James and John, we can always find good reasons for
striking down the ones who have struck us. We can always hide
our urge for revenge behind the cloak of so-called righteous
indignation. If necessary, we can almost always find historical
precedent for reprisals. We, like Jesus, angry followers, can
strengthen our reasons for rage by alluding to an Elijah or other

famous heroes. Sometimes, we modern Sons of Thunder even try to find a rationale for rampaging by appealing to Scripture. James and John propped up their case for retaliating by referring to 2 Kings 1:9–17, and we often try to veil our vengeful thoughts by claiming to stand on "religious principle" or a biblical proof-test.

It is easy to settle accounts by punishing the other. Jesus, however, rules out this easy settlement for His followers. With Jesus, there is no such word as *enemy*. He has expunged the term from our vocabularies as a word which we can use against anyone else. The reason: Jesus Christ has called friend that one we label enemy. He pronounces them subjects for concern rather than objects of contempt.

"Violence and communication are mutually exclusive," psychiatrist Rollo May observes. Striking down despised Samaritans with fire, Jesus knew, cut off any possibility of communication and reconciliation. The ultimate congeniality between all persons—Jew and Samaritan included—which Jesus called His Kingdom, means a new arrangement between adversaries. His Kingdom—the new arrangement—brings freedom and hope for everyone. Contempt and contention have no place in the community which Jesus Christ's Kingdom is arranging.

A settlement-house nurse in New York recently asked a mother of thirteen children which of her children she loves the most. The mother sensibly replied, "The one I love the most? The one who is sick, until he gets well. The one who is away, until he gets home." So also with God?

Vengeance may crush the wrongdoer. But it does not conquer him. God means to conquer the wrongdoer with love! "For the Son of man is not come to destroy men's lives, but to save them . . ." Jesus reminded the pair of vengeful disciples (Luke 9:56 KJV).

Those Samaritans? Save *them?* They are not worth it!

That's God's problem with everyone. With James and John. With you and me. He, however, has decided that we all *are* worth it. He is well aware of the high cost of loving—more conscious of it than anyone else. Yet—He has paid the price. On a hill, outside the city, when that Person who insisted on saving men's lives hung on an instrument of execution and torture, God indicated once and for all that He puts incalculable value on Samaritans, on James and John, on you and me. "Greater love has no man than this, that a man lay down his life for his friends" (John 15:13); our friendship means that we are worth dying for.

Therefore, you and I treat others not the way in which they treat us, but the way God treats us. We repay hostility with forgiveness.

Love is not "other-worldly" but very "this-worldly." Jesus acknowledged that this world is very evil. We, too, know that we are surrounded by evil people bent on destruction; we are beset by odious persons diabolically determined to hurt. Jesus knew what evil was all about, and so do we Christians. His career was a series of showdowns with those demonically obsessed to dehumanize everyone. He understood the hellishness of evil better than anyone. We, His followers, need never put on nice-Nellyish mannerisms or rose-tinted lenses about evil's pervasive powers. He has shown us our own real nature enough to permit us to be realistic about life in this world. He frees us from false optimism about human nature.

Love is more than inertly refraining from taking reprisals against evil ones. Choosing not to retaliate can be a form of copping out. Christian love, far from being negative, is positive. Christian love, far from being passive, is active. Love means going out on a limb for the other, hateful and despicable though he may be—just as the Loving One hung on a limb for us. Love means seeking out those needing love, those incapable of showing love—those unable to care must first receive caring. We love because He first loved us. The worse the hatred, the more the other needs our love. This kind of concern comes out of strength, not out of weakness.

"The Son of man is not come to destroy men's lives but to save them" (Luke 9:56 KJV). Caring—Christ-style—neutralizes the horrifying powers of vengefulness. Loving—Christ-style—counteracts the deathly effects of loathing.

The only fire which we call down on anyone is the fire of the Holy Spirit. The purifying, warming, empowering brilliance of the Flaming Presence is fire enough!

That fire did come on Samaritan villages. Significantly, God's flame, Spirit-Fire, came because of John, one of the Sons of Thunder who once had pleaded with Jesus to be allowed to summon God to scorch a certain Samaritan village.

What happened to John and James? Obviously, they learned that Jesus ignited a different kind of fire, the unquenchable flame of forgiving love. These two disciples turned into new kinds of firebrands. Instead of demanding the fire of retribution, they blazed with the kind of fire which ultimately burns through and through, refining, tempering, changing even the hardest, most hateful person.

> Beloved, never avenge yourselves, but leave it to the wrath of God. . . ." If your enemy is hungry, feed him; if he is thirsty, give him drink; for by so doing you will heap burning coals up on his head." Do not be overcome with evil, but overcome evil with good.
>
> Romans 12:19–21

11

Peter,
who tried to lose himself in work

David Livingstone, the missionary-explorer, was heartbroken and despondent as he dug the grave under a baobab tree in steaming Africa to bury his wife. For the first time in his life, he confided in his journal, he admitted that he would be content to die. He patted the last shovelful of earth on the grave and resumed his work. Overcome with grief and loneliness, Livingstone tried to lose himself in his work. "The sweat of one's brow is no longer a curse," he wrote. "It proves a tonic."

"I'm going back to fishing," Simon Peter announced after Jesus' Crucifixion. Work, Peter hoped, would be a kind of therapy.

Peter and Jesus' other followers were emotionally devastated by Jesus' death. They could not understand how their Friend and Leader could end His career so ignominiously.

Although it had only been a few years, to Peter it seemed that he had been with Jesus all of his life. Perhaps it was because everything important in Peter's life had taken place after he had joined Jesus' company.

Peter had sometimes remembered the cost. Although he had not tallied up the total, Peter knew that selling his share of the boat, the nets, the fishing gear represented a considerable sacrifice. Peter also remembered that forsaking fishing to follow Jesus meant missing many good catches on the Sea of Galilee. Every night he was not in the boat, Peter occasionally thought, amounted to giving up part of his income. However, Peter willingly traded security for salvation. Being with Jesus was worth any sacrifice.

Peter had never met anyone like the magnetic Nazarene. Peter joyfully hurled himself into assisting Jesus' ministry. At first, the response was gratifying. Peter proudly noted that hundreds and hundreds thronged to hear Jesus. Caught up in the excitement of being near a popular hero, Peter tried not to hear Jesus' private conversations about suffering for others with him and other close companions. In fact, Peter wished that Jesus would not talk so much about sacrifice.

Peter liked Jesus' words about the coming Kingdom. Kingdom-talk was heady stuff! What pictures it conjured up! Peter fantasized that Jesus' Kingdom would feature all the pomp and splendor of a royal court.

Privately, Peter began to understand that Jesus was the long-awaited Messiah. Peter, however, carefully kept this opinion to himself. Even Andrew, his brother, had no inkling of Peter's ideas of Jesus' messiahship.

In his reveries, Peter occasionally pictured himself in Jesus' palace, enjoying a position of power and prominence. After all, Peter assured himself, popular tradition insisted that the Messiah would be a second David. Would not the Messiah-Deliverer at least match King David in prestige and pageantry? Surely the second David's personal retinue would be entitled to some of the trappings of a kingly court.

Although opposition to Jesus by the authorities began to grow intense, Peter felt no anxiety. He was confident that Jesus would put down all opposition. When spies and agents from wily, remorseless Herod (the puppet-king who ruled Galilee for Rome) made it too hazardous for Jesus to stay in the area, Peter didn't worry. Jesus' hour was coming. Peter, however, still had not confided to anyone his certainty that Jesus was the Messiah.

One day after Jesus and the others had left Galilee to escape Herod, they were approaching the town of Caesarea-Philippi. Peter listened intently to Jesus' conversation as they walked. When Peter heard Jesus' question, "But who do you say that I am?" Peter blurted what he had been thinking for some time, "You are the Christ, the Son of the living God" (Matthew 16:16).

What a glow Peter had felt at that time! Peter recalled that Jesus had confirmed that, indeed, He was the Christ, the Anointed One of Israel!

Although Jesus had chided Peter shortly afterward for trying to persuade Jesus that He would not have to suffer for Israel, Peter chose to remember the messiahship part. Excitement mounted as the party progressed toward Jerusalem, and Peter sensed that Jesus' great days were about to come.

Jerusalem! Peter thrilled at the prospect of Jesus proclaiming His rule in the great capital. When Jesus unmistakably declared His messiahship by riding into the holy city on the back of a she-ass, Peter watched with joy. The bystanders jubilantly responded, Peter observed. Cheering pilgrims spread branches and garments in the road before Jesus, in recognition that Jesus was the Messiah! Jesus' cause was firing the crowds!

The following day, Peter joined Jesus on a visit to the temple. Peter was delighted when Jesus asserted His authority by moving the livestock and coin-changers out of the area reserved for prayer by outsiders. Peter knew that Jesus was the man of the hour—the person everyone was talking about in Jerusalem. Soon, Peter reminded himself, everyone would bow in subjection to the Messiah! What glorious days lay ahead!

Peter, puzzled at Jesus' repeated talk of suffering, nonetheless felt certain that Jesus as conquering Hero-Messiah would sweep aside all opposition. Peter frankly did not understand Jesus' actions and words as the Twelve gathered in an upper room for the pre-Passover celebration. Although Judas had soured and defected, Peter did not believe that one traitor would stop Jesus' destiny.

Peter confidently walked with Jesus into Gethsemane, the Place of the Oil Press where they planned to sleep. He heard Jesus' warning to His followers that He, the Shepherd, would be struck and that they, His flock, would scatter. Indignant, Peter answered, "Though they all fall away because of you, I will never fall away" (Matthew 26:33). Peter stoutly announced his loyalty would never falter. "Lord, I am ready to go with you to prison and to death" (Luke 22:33).

Peter's rhetoric had a brave ring. He secretly felt pleased

with his noble words. When Jesus quietly remarked that Peter would deny Him three times before the first rooster would crow at dawn, Peter loudly reaffirmed his willingness to go to any lengths for Jesus. "If I must die with you [Peter insisted], I will not deny you" (Mark 14:31).

Jesus somberly looked at Peter.

When the little group came to the place where they would stay for the night, Peter, James, and John, the trio always closest to Jesus, prepared to stretch out under an olive tree near Jesus and catch some sleep. Peter and the other two heard Jesus ask them to sit up with Him for a while. Peter readily agreed; James and John likewise said that they'd sit up while Jesus prayed. Using a tree as a backrest, Peter sat down. He heard Jesus starting to pray, and could tell what a struggle Jesus was going through. Peter closed his eyes and took a deep breath. Jesus' voice seemed to grow fainter. Suddenly Peter was aware that Jesus' voice was loud again, and was speaking to him.

"Simon," Jesus said, using the old name instead of the nickname Peter. "Simon, are you asleep? [Jesus asked in disbelief!] Could you not watch one hour? Watch and pray that you may not enter into temptation; the spirit indeed is willing, but the flesh is weak" (Mark 14:37, 38).

Chagrined, Peter realized that he had dozed off. Mumbling apologies and promises, Peter assured Jesus that he would stay awake with Him this time.

Minutes later, Peter stirred as he heard his name again. Dismayed, he knew that he had drifted off to sleep a second time. He did not know what to say to Jesus. Peter resolved to watch and overheard the broken cries as Jesus agonized in prayer. Peter briefly wondered why that night was such a struggle for Jesus. As he pondered, he slipped into sleep a third time.

The next twenty-four hours were the most ghastly Peter ever experienced. Everything went wrong. Suddenly, all the forces of hellishness seemed to converge to destroy Jesus the Messiah.

Peter was snapped into wakefulness by Jesus' voice, and sheepishly admitted to himself that he had failed to keep his promise to sit up with his Friend. Simon Peter quickly realized, however, that trouble was approaching. Through the trees, he saw the procession of flickering torches and heard the clink of metal. Armed men—guards! At that hour, an armed detachment of police meant only one thing, namely that Jesus was marked for arrest. Swinging to his feet, Peter prepared to defend his Messiah.

He watched in astonishment as Judas brazenly marched up and gave the customary greeting of a disciple to a beloved rabbi. Peter wondered what Judas had in mind. Suddenly it became clear. Peter saw that Judas greeted Jesus in order to point him out to the guards. When one of the guards stepped forward to seize Jesus, Peter angrily snatched the weapon he had quietly brought along and started to swing widely. He slashed at the guard, gashing the man badly on the side of the head.

"No more of this!" Jesus sternly commanded Peter (Luke 22:51). "Put your sword back into its place; for all who take the sword will perish by the sword" (Matthew 26:52).

Peter felt as if he had been pierced with hot steel. He stared dumbly at the man he had wounded, than at Jesus who was staunching the flow of blood and gently attending to the guard's nearly severed ear.

Turning again to Peter, Jesus asked, "Do you think that I cannot appeal to my Father, and he will at once send me more than twelve legions of angels? But how then should the scriptures be fulfilled . . . ?" (Matthew 26:53).

Peter glumly realized that his show of force was a cheap bit of bravado, and totally out of keeping with Jesus' way. He dumbly watched the guards grab Jesus' arms and tightly wrap ropes around Him. It suddenly occurred to Peter that it was dangerous to get mixed up with a patrol making an arrest. He shrank back into the shadows and darkness of the trees.

When the detachment of temple police moved out of the area with Jesus in tow, Peter followed a safe distance behind. He tried to appear to be a late-returning pilgrim, nonchalantly wandering into the city after an evening party in an outlying village. He kept a careful several dozen paces between himself and the arrest party, far enough to avoid suspicion but near enough to see where they were taking Jesus. He felt better; he told himself that he was behaving coolly in adversity.

Peter watched the group disappear into the mansion of the ex-high priest, the real power behind temple politics. Peter noticed some of the servants and a few bystanders warming their hands around a charcoal brazier in the courtyard. Observing that people casually came and went in the area, Peter ambled up to the small cluster of people gathered around the glowing charcoal. He assured himself that it was so dark that no one could detect him. Besides, people from the street sometimes walked over to rub their hands over the coals for a few minutes before wandering on.

Peter tried to act casual when one of the group around the tiny fire, a hefty woman from the high priest's kitchen, stared intently at him. Peter wondered if she had noticed his anxious glances toward the house where Jesus had been taken.

"This man also was with him" (Luke 22:56), the woman snickered to her companions, and pointed a fat thumb toward Peter.

Incensed that he should be suspected by a loud-voiced dishwasher, Peter huffed, "Woman, I do not know him!" (Luke 22:57).

His vigorous denial silenced the woman. Relieved that the crisis had past, Peter looked again at the doors through which Jesus had been led. He listened as the conversation kept returning to Jesus but avoided making any comments. He was disconcerted to hear someone else accuse him of connections with the prisoner.

"You also are one of them" (Luke 22:58), a man gruffly observed, turning to Peter for confirmation.

Determined to avoid having his cover blown, Peter instantly replied, "Man, I'm not" (Luke 22:59).

Nervously, Peter walked away from the circle. The faint orange glow of the firepot silhouetted the few people still standing in the courtyard and provided the only blur of light in the black night. Peter shivered. It was cold. The hour was late. Noticing that the group huddled around the charcoal had grown silent, Peter figured that they were sleepy enough to ignore him. He unobtrusively slipped into the warm zone near the coals. To his relief, the small talk subsided to an occasional comment about the cold or the Passover holiday. Suddenly shouts and laughter rang from behind the doors. Peter and the group outside could tell that guards were taunting the prisoner. The talk around the charcoal fire returned to the topic of the Galilean rabbi inside the mansion. Peter wondered when Jesus would emerge through the doors and tried to picture precisely what was transpiring inside. His thoughts were abruptly interrupted.

"Certainly this man also was with him," a man across from him muttered to his neighbor as he eyed Peter. The two had been holding a private conversation about Peter's identity. Referring to Peter's gutteral accent, the first speaker added, "for he is a Galilean" (Luke 22:59).

Peter exploded angrily. Ugly fisherman's curses tumbled from his lips. The disciple who a few hours earlier had promised loyalty to Jesus to his dying gasp swore, "I do not know the man" (Matthew 26:74).

Silence followed Peter's vehement denial. Somewhere in the distance, a rooster crowed. Just as the last insistent notes trilled away, the door of the high priest's house opened. The brilliance of the torches inside the room illuminated Jesus, who turned and looked toward Peter.

Suddenly Peter realized the enormity of his acts. He had denied Jesus. Exactly as Jesus had warned, Peter had denied Him before cockcrow! And not just one denial, but three. First, Peter had denied knowing Jesus. Then he had denied being a disciple. Finally, Peter had denied having any knowledge of Jesus whatsoever!

Hastily, Peter turned and fled. Outside the courtyard, Peter suddenly threw his hands against his face, and uncontrollably broke into sobbing. He leaned against the wall, his huge shoulders shaking, and wept bitterly.

A few hours later, a drained and depressed Peter regained his composure enough to watch the execution squad herd its prisoner through the streets. Too frightened to want to attract attention, Peter huddled as anonymously as possible on the outside edge of the crowd. He avoided speaking, to prevent his Galilean accent from arousing suspicion. He preserved a discreet distance from the doomed Jesus and His executioners.

Far enough away to avoid danger for himself, Peter watched the death penalty carried out. Even at a distance, nailing a human to a cross was a sickening sight. Numbly, Peter stood and waited. He saw his Friend writhe in His death throes. Three hours later, it was all over. The Figure on the cross had given a few last gasps and twitches, then had sagged, grotesque and broken, with an army spear protruding from His side. Peter later remembered some others lowering the now-gray corpse into an improvised body bag, and hauling the battered, blood-ied thing to a cave-tomb down the hill.

"Every man for himself," Peter thought. "I had better get out of here. Who knows? I may be next on the list for arrest and death! I'm a marked man around Jerusalem. Back to Galilee for me."

When Jesus had died, in a sense Peter had died, too. Peter felt terribly guilty. All hope of forgiveness and being right with Jesus his Friend had perished when Jesus had expired. Disillu-sioned, scared, and ashamed, Peter skulked out of Jerusalem. Life seemed to have ceased. Only darkness and death seemed to be the ultimate realities.

Galilee seemed to be the last island of sanity and safety for Peter. He wearily noticed that several of the other members of the Twelve had also scurried north to their old familiar fishing village. When they met, they talked despondently. Without Jesus, life was empty and pointless. Listless, they watched some of their old buddies preparing to put out to fish one evening.

Peter and the others knew that they had to subsist in some way. "I am going fishing" (John 21:3), Peter blurted.

Peter and his mates, all former followers of Jesus, borrowed a boat, hurriedly rounded up nets and gear, and pushed out.

Back to fishing. It made sense to Peter and the others. After the emotional intensity of the previous two or three years, par-ticularly the crisis of Jesus' disgrace and death, they welcomed the placid, comfortable life of being plain fishermen again. The only crises they would have to face as fishermen would be an occasional night of nasty weather or a run of poor catches. All that Peter desired was the security of a few good hauls of fish each week, income enough to pay his debts and taxes, and to be left alone.

And fishing seemed to be an antidote for the grief and guilt which Peter carried. Jesus was dead. Peter was certain that he would never again have any fellowship with Jesus. Worse, Peter remembered the ways in which he had failed Jesus. The memory of falling asleep at Gethsemane when Jesus had asked him to sit up with Him pained deeply. More painful—so much so that Peter's throat choked and his eyes brimmed every time he remembered—was the recollection of the night he had denied Jesus. Peter despaired of himself each time he recalled his disgraceful failure that night in the courtyard. Not once, he reminded himself, but *three* times he had denied the One whom he had promised he would follow to the end.

The end had come for Jesus, Peter grimly told himself. The end had come for Peter, too. For everybody. For Peter, there was no future. Nor much of a present. With no future, Peter tried desperately to lunge into his past. Peter turned to fishing to recover some illusion of an innocent earlier life. With the kind of despair for today and tomorrow which Peter felt, a return to the nets and boats was a desperate attempt to preserve his sanity as well as his skin.

The snap of the wind, the slap of the waves, the smell of the equipment and the feel of oars and lines in Peter's hands felt good. After all the uncertainly and tragedy, there was something refreshingly solid and reassuring about working the nets again. Expertly, he payed out the net in a big arc between two boats. As the darkness settled, Peter prepared himself for the cold by struggling into his rough fisherman's smock. He knew from long experience on the lake that the fish ran best at night. Besides, at daybreak he could take their freshly caught haul immediately to the fish markets.

Peter and the others worked the boats, dragging the net into a gradually closing circle to trap their catch. Each time they performed the operation, however, they found their net empty of any good fish. Disgusted, they repeated the maneuver time after time. They shifted to different areas on the lake but still tugged in an empty net.

They could not seem to do anything right. Determined to be successful fishermen, they caught nothing. Years later, recalling that night on the water, they nodded and reminded each other that without Jesus they couldn't do a thing. The disciples of the presumed-dead-for-good Jesus mistakenly thought that they could act alone the night they returned to fishing.

Chilly and depressed, Peter and his fellow fishermen wearily worked their boats through the mists toward the shore where they had often talked with Jesus. The faintest signs of dawn had just begun to appear over the cliffs to the east.

"Say, you boys haven't caught anything by any chance, have you?" someone called from shore.

Peter and the others, assuming it was someone wanting to buy something, grumbled to themselves. A paying customer on shore, but nothing to sell! Wearily, they called back that they have had no luck.

"Try the other side of the boat!" the voice from shore shouted.

Peter and the rest knew that sometimes a person on shore could spot a shoal of fish. They allowed themselves to be directed by the stranger. Suddenly, Peter and his friends discovered that they were astonishingly, embarrassingly successful.

Old salt John, the Gospel writer, never forgot a good catch and never landed a haul of fish without counting them. When he wrote the account of that evening sometime later, he recorded the exact number—153 good fish, one of his largest catches. John also remembered the surprise and relief which everyone felt that the net withstood the strain of such a heavy haul without ripping.

Peter, John, and the others in the boats wondered who the stranger on shore was. It was too far and too dark to tell by looking. As they heaved at the oars to encircle the enormous shoal of fish they had suddenly trapped, they mused that their unexpected direction and success seemed to be a sign. Who could direct such a work but . . . ? Their sudden good fortune could only be attributed to Jesus! John deduced that the voice from the beach could only belong to Jesus. "It is the Lord!" (John 21:7) he whispered to Peter.

"Although John had the keener insight, Peter had the greater ardor," the Slavic scholar Euthymius observed centuries later. Gathering his rough fisherman's smock between his legs and tucking the tails into a piece of rope around his waist, Peter impulsively jumped overboard and excitedly splashed ashore. Peter could not wait for the nets to be hauled or the boats to come around and be rowed toward shore. Jesus was alive!

The last thing that Peter or any of the others ever expected was to see Jesus alive again. Yet, Jesus stood there on the beach that day.

The Resurrection was not a body-snatch by the disciples to fool the public. Easter was no "Passover plot" to hoodwink the public or deceive the gullible. Emphatically, Peter and the others saw no apparition. The Resurrection was no haunted-house act, no back-from-the-grave chiller-thriller where hyped-up imaginations *think* they see someone returned from the dead. Nor was the Resurrection a myth or symbol of a purely subjective spiritual experSence.

Instead, the Resurrection was an event—an actuality. The appearance of Jesus alive to the disciples was a fact just as real as the Crucifixion.

The disciples never tried to make the Resurrection of Jesus Christ sound plausible or reasonable. On the contrary, they always admitted that they were shocked by Jesus' appearance. They fully realized that many would scoff, that others would be patronizingly skeptical. Peter and a group of hard-headed, guilt-ridden men found themselves surprised in the midst of their everyday chores. Jesus lived!

The Resurrection of Jesus was God's *no!* to Peter's announcement, "I am going fishing." In a sense, it was God's refusal to permit Peter to bury his guilt and grief through work. Peter planned to forget his failure through fishing. Peter assumed that he could ease the ache and loneliness by a job and possessions. For a man who despaired over the future, going back to past haunts and habits seemed the sensible course. God, however, raised up Jesus Christ, rehabilitating and reinstating Peter.

Peter, a nickname meaning rocky, seemed an absurd name for a man who showed so few granitelike characteristics during

Jesus' final days on earth. As shifting and unstable as a sandbar, the man named Rocky who planned to eke out his remaining years on the lake was served breakfast by the Risen Lord.

A meal meant a sacred bond among those eating together. Sharing bread and fish symbolized Jesus' desire to renew His relationship with Simon, nicknamed Peter. It was as if Jesus said to the big-talking, fair-weather follower who had denied Him and failed Him, *So you've blown it, Peter. Badly. Completely. You know it, and I know it. But, Peter, I mean to be with you! I intend to renew our relationship. And I want you to understand that this relationship is with the Father-God. This is why He has brought Me back to you, Peter, and to the others who failed Me. Through Me, He gives you a new beginning. He restores that relationship which you and the others broke off. That relationship cannot be severed—ever. Not even by death!*

Every October 31, at precisely 1:26 P.M., a group gathers at Machpelah Cemetery in Queens, New York, at the grave of Harry Houdini, the master magician, showman, and escape artist. Although Houdini died in 1926, a pathetic group of magicians try to perpetuate his memory by assembling annually at the hour and day of his death. Their ceremony remains the same. At exactly 1:26, a magician's wand is broken in two, and the pieces are dropped on Houdini's grave, symbolizing the broken prowess of the great magician.

The powers of every person are snapped off at death, except with Jesus Christ. Even the grave cannot break *His* powers! Nor will His relationship with Peter—and with us—ever be broken. The Resurrection is God's mighty *no* to depression and death. For Peter and all others who sigh, "Nothing in life for me but work," God raised Christ as His complete, massive rehabilitation program.

Pointing to Peter's boat, nets, tackle, and gear, Jesus bluntly demanded, "Simon, son of John, do you love me more than these?" (John 21:15). Was Peter willing to put Jesus ahead of a steady job, a successful career, a safe future, and certain profits? Did Peter care more about the security and certainty of his old life as a fisherman than his calling as an apostle? Jesus pushed Peter from lip service to a deep-down evaluation of his commitments. He forced Peter to rearrange his plans and priorities.

"Do you love . . ." Jesus repeated. He persisted in making Peter understand that caring was the bond which they held in common and what kept them together.

"Do you care about Me?" Jesus in effect asked Peter.

Peter responded, "You know I'm Your friend."

"Do you care about Me?" Jesus asked again.

Flustered, Peter replied, "Yes, of course I'm Your friend."

"Are you My friend?" Jesus demanded a third time.

Peter, hurt that Jesus repeated His questions about loyalties three times, winced. He started to make another of his loud, brash promises—but stopped. He remembered. Three times, he recalled, he denied Jesus. Three times Jesus had asked whether Peter cared about his Friend. Peter suddenly understood that Jesus' threefold question was a symbolic undoing of Peter's threefold denial.

"Feed my lambs. Tend my sheep" (*see* vs. 15, 16), Jesus smiled, reinstating Peter to his former position of trust and authority. The Risen Lord reinstalled Peter to lead God's people, to act on behalf of the Shepherd.

Peter remembered that Jesus embodied the words, "The Lord is my Shepherd, I shall not want." He grasped that Jesus was insisting that he, Peter, be a personification of the Good Shepherd!

Peter solemnly acknowledged that he understood. He was to be an undershepherd. He was to stay with the helpless, the hurting, the frightened, the straying, the disabled, the confused. These, Peter comprehended, were Christ's "sheep," and these were now Peter's responsibility.

"Tend my sheep!" Peter smiled joyfully when he heard the words. He knew that he had duties in life far more important than peddling fish. Most important, he understood that Jesus trusted Peter so much that He was leaving His flock in Peter's care!

Peter accepted God's *no* to his fishing proposal, knowing that God had greater plans in store. He remembered Jesus' words at the time the Master had called him from the boat and nets the first time, at the start of Jesus' ministry, "Follow me, and I will make you fishers of men" (Matthew 4:19).

Peter's fishing career was interrupted twice by the Lord. He finally learned, however, that Christ's "Follow Me!" was God's great *yes!* And in following Jesus, Peter found forgiveness and a future!

12

A Beggar,
who pleaded for a handout

He was one of nature's cruel jokes. Totally unable to look after himself, he was not able to sit up or even to be propped up. He was so completely paralyzed that he had to be carried everywhere and laid down flat.

Orthopedic surgeons today, examining the case history as recorded by Luke the physician, indicate this man could have been a victim of congenital rickets, or meningitis, or "brittle bones," or cerebral palsy in a severe, spastic, quadraplegic form, or *spina biffida*—paralyzed from the waist down, or broken neck at the time of delivery, or perhaps born with the spinal cord's roots on the outside. Any of these could have caused paralysis. In addition, medical experts point out, the man would have suffered progressive deformity through the years.

For over forty years—all his best years—the man knew helplessness. He realized that he was a burden to others. Helpless, he often grew irritated at having to be carried everywhere, but resigned himself to being dependent on family or neighbors. He perceived that others resented the way his condition intruded on their plans and disturbed their routine.

Aware that he was a nuisance, the cripple also sensed that he was an embarrassment to everyone. He had also discovered years earlier that others did not like seeing him because he made them feel guilty for having health, or guilty for not doing much about him. The paralytic had grudgingly accepted the cruel sentence of being doomed to an existence which would cause resentment and problems for everyone.

Today, society would sweep this kind of patient off to the limbo of a distant institution. In the first century, society grudgingly permitted him to beg.

Someone had tacked together some poles and heavy cloth for a stretcherlike litter for the man. Each morning except the Sabbath, a few neighbor boys hauled the litter holding the paralytic through the streets to a busy intersection. Deposited on the street corner, the man whiled away the day by cadging handouts. Each evening, just before sundown, the neighbor boys returned to carry him back to his tiny cubicle in a filthy back alley in the poorest section of Jerusalem.

He depended completely on whatever small change he could beg. If he had a good day, he collected enough to buy some bread, olives, and perhaps some fruit for his evening meal, hoarding enough of one of the flat barley loaves to munch as breakfast the following day. Once in a while, he received enough coins to stop at a restaurant stall for a bowl of hot vegetable stew and to give the neighbor boys a small tip.

There were also days when he could scrounge nothing, days when sheets of cold rain slashed at Jerusalem and nobody wanted to stop to give alms to any beggar, or days when the wind whipped the dust and sand into a billion tiny stinging projectiles, and traffic practically stopped. On those days, the paralytic went hungry.

Rain or shine, six days a week, he followed the same desperate, dreary routine of trying to subsist. He had long since abandoned hope of any change in his condition or circumstances after forty years of pain and paralysis. His expectations had been scaled down so that he hoped for nothing more than enough coins to permit him to eat that night. His horizons had shrunk to the edge of his begging bowl.

In recent times, he had stationed himself in the temple area. He knew, of course, he could not be taken inside the areas where Israelites worshiped because there were strict rules prohibiting cripples being carried past the Court of the Women.

The paralytic resigned himself to never being able to worship properly. Sometimes, he wondered why his religion would prevent him from approaching God. As a hopeless cripple, he knew that he would never be able to walk into the Court of the Israelites and present his offering. He painfully realized that he would never have the satisfaction of sensing that the Eternal One acknowledged his prayers and sacrifice. Crippled beggars, he concluded, were apparently not welcome in God's presence. The man on the litter sighed that he would never be close to the Almighty or close to others. He was walled off not only by his infirmity but also by regulations. The cripple was a religious nonentity as well as a community nobody. He knew well, after years of lying helplessly prone, that the universe barely tolerated useless nuisances who wailed for alms.

Years of experience had taught him the strategic locations for begging. The best places, of course, were along heavily travelled routes or beside busy public entrances. Whenever he could beat out the others from the horde of beggars, the paralytic had himself deposited next to the portal of the Court of Israel. Everyone conceded that this was the choice place to beg. Every male Jew going and coming to worship had to pass near him. The magnificent bronze doors, the Nicanor Gate nicknamed Beautiful Gate, inspired a certain awe so that worshipers quieted their voices as they approached. The paralytic and the other mendicants by the Beautiful Gate took advantage of the hush, knowing that their howls for baksheesh would be heard better.

The cripple stationed himself by the Beautiful Gate not only because it was one of the busiest thoroughfares, but because many worshipers had some spare change after buying their dove or other offering. Furthermore, almsgiving was held in high regard. What better place to jab the consciences of religious people to give alms than at the entrance of the place of worship? The paralyzed beggar had shrewdly figured all the angles.

After forty years of pleading for handouts, he had learned to pick out the likeliest givers. Out-of-towners, he concluded, seemed to be a softer touch. Tourists always carried a little money. Strangers from the country usually had never seen a case quite as pathetic as his. They weren't like the Jerusalem people who had grown blasé after seeing his twisted, useless form stretched out on the street and so many other disabled spongers. Country folk had not been numbed by the sight of malformed bodies and did not have the crust of indifference that city dwellers had. The crippled beggar observed that the pilgrims from the villages came to Jerusalem with religion on their minds, and therefore were more inclined to feel sorry for him and to reach into their money pouches.

The paralytic immediately noticed the two men from Galilee approaching the Beautiful Gate that afternoon. He could tell by their voices and their powerful fishermen's builds that they were from up in the north country. It was during the evening rush hour, the time when people leaving work were hurrying home for the end-of-the-day chores and stopping off in the temple for quick prayer and praises. In spite of the throngs passing in and out of the Gate, the beggar picked out the two Galilean fishermen as the likeliest marks for a handout.

He opened his mouth and began his piercing whine for alms. If he could wheedle a couple of extra copper coins from them, he thought that he might be able to afford a helping of steaming lentil soup that evening. He was too smart, however, to beg for copper money. (Ask for copper stuff and get nothing; therefore ask for silver and gold, and get copper! And don't just ask once. Keep on pleading. And sound insistent.) Mechanically, the paralytic put on his shrill, unrelenting pitch.

"Alms! For the sake of the Merciful One, give me some silver or gold," he cried. "Oh, please! *Please!* Some alms for this helpless wretch! Some coins that I may have something to eat tonight."

The beggar knew that his two prospects were coming closer, but he did not bother to look up. He stepped up the tone and the volume of his appeal for spare change. It was an impersonal request—like a form letter—for a dole which he had made so many hundreds of times that it sounded insincere. His spiel was obviously overrehearsed. The cripple did not care; he played the percentages. He had learned that if he pestered enough people long enough, he would usually pick up enough small change to eat for another day. All he wanted was a couple of coppers. He didn't care for approval; he didn't hope for acceptance. He had long since abandoned all pretense of dignity.

"Give me just one gold coin! One gold coin, please! Or even a silver coin! I beg of you! Have mercy on this poor cripple! Please, some alms. For the love of God, let me have even one silver coin!" the paralytic keened.

He paid little attention when the two men stopped. At least, he told himself, they hadn't stepped around him, pretending not to notice him, as so many did. He also wearily observed that they hadn't dropped anything into his bowl. What were they waiting for—others to take notice that they were going to give alms? The beggar cynically recalled the dozens of episodes when big givers waited for an audience. Almsgiving, he remembered with a sour scowl, brought public approval and an easier conscience for a cheap price. If these two prospects wanted to delay their giving until others took notice, he would oblige. Meanwhile, he kept up the pressure. He continued to plead.

"Look at us!"

The command interrupted the beggar's wails like a sharp slap. Startled, the paralyzed man fell silent. What was this? he thought. Who were these men? What did they want—additional credit for their couple of measly coppers? Or were they temple authorities officiously getting ready to tell him to move out of the way and stop blocking traffic?

All he demanded from life was a decent meal. All he pleaded for was a bit of cash. His prayers to God, his requests from others focused exclusively on a full stomach for one more evening.

And God in effect said *no!*

Sometimes God says *no* to our requests because He has something better in mind for us.

"Look at us" (Acts 3:4), the two strangers from Galilee ordered.

Suspiciously, the paralytic jerked his head up to look at the Galileans. He silently cursed the pain from the exertion to look at them. (*C'mon*, he said to himself, let me have a coin or two. If I had only half of what you have in your purse, I'd be happy for the rest of my life. All I need is more money, and everything will be fine. A couple of gold and silver coins would really fix me up!)

One of the Galileans spoke in his rough, gutteral north-country accent. "I have no silver and gold . . ." (Acts 3:6).

(Just what I might have thought, mused the crippled beggar. One of those flat-broke fanatics from the hills who comes down to the holy city, and thinks he has to preach to me or pray over me. No thanks! Just don't bother me. Move on, and get out of the way so I can put the touch on someone else.)

"I have no silver and gold [the Galilean insisted], but I give you what I have. . . ."

(*What you have!* snorted the helpless man to himself. What good is what you have if it isn't in the form of hard cash? If what you have can't be jangled in a purse, you don't have much. The man who has money has everything.)

". . . but I give you what I have," the Galilean insisted.

(Here comes the sermon on "patience" or "suffering", the helpless man sighed irritably. This religious crackpot will give me what he has, and that's probably a headful of windy prayers. That's a great help when what I need is good silver and gold coins and lots of them.)

"IN THE NAME OF JESUS CHRIST OF NAZARETH, WALK!" (*See* Acts 3:6).

Suddenly and unexpectedly, the beggar found himself gripped by the right hand. He felt the powerful arms of one of the Galileans tugging him upward. Too astonished to resist, the cripple realized that the other was raising him to his feet!

The next minutes were so packed with excitement that the paralyzed beggar never figured out exactly how everything happened. Incredibly, he discovered that he could stand. Feet and ankle bones, once distorted and misshapen "were made strong" according to physician-author Luke, using the medical word for limp, useless appendages becoming firm and strengthened. His body, which had resembled a large, ugly wounded insect, unaccountably strengthened and surged with strength! He could stand! He wiggled his fingers and toes. He excitedly jiggled. He laughed, yet found tears pouring down his cheeks. Shaking his arms, he tentatively took a couple of steps. Then he jumped. Joyfully breaking into a spontaneous dance, the man shouted praises to God.

When his benefactors, the two Galileans named Peter and

John, started to move into the place of worship, the beggar attached himself to them. He tried to walk sedately, but he was so intoxicated with the ecstatic gift he had just received that every few steps he suddenly jigged with glee! "Praise the Lord! I can walk!" he announced exuberantly.

The hopeless case on the litter by the entrance to the temple was one of the first to discover that Christians care about bodies as well as souls. Indeed, he learned, Peter and John and their companions had a concern for others' needs, physical and spiritual. The onetime paralytic didn't think much about it at the time, but he detected that Christians know that every person is a bundle of hurts of all kinds. And those Galileans, the beggar quickly found, meant to move to meet those hurts.

These strong fishermen were poor in purse, the beggar knew. But their power! They were millionaires in strength!

The onetime paralytic recalled their words. *"In the name of Jesus Christ of Nazareth, walk!"* The source of the Galileans' power lay not in themselves but in the name of Jesus Christ of Nazareth.

Name equalled power in that culture. To do something in someone's "name" meant acting with the authority and in the capacity of a representative of the person whose name was used. The beggar understood that Peter and John operated "in the name" or carried the authority of Jesus Christ himself.

Through Jesus Christ's deputies, in the strong name of this builder from Nazareth, the helpless mendicant who had been born paralyzed found his life rebuilt! He had pleaded for coins, certain that more wealth would solve all his problems. He had been refused his request for funds. Instead of receiving a generous dole for continued helplessness, the crippled beggar discovered that God blessed him with health for dignity and independence. He also found that God's *no* is sometimes a prelude to something better for us.

The destitute man, who had eked out his forty years on the margin of society, learned to his surprise that his new found friends brought him into the community. With Peter and John, the ex-cripple circulated with others. He was no longer alienated. No longer a supine freak, he did not have to endure the curious stares of bystanders. No longer a helpless indigent, he did not have to accept subhuman subsistence from a reluctant society. He was accepted as a person! He was part of the community! He could work, he could mingle as an equal. He could buy and sell, give and take, come and go with the same freedom and responsibilities as any other person in Jerusalem—thanks to the Name of Jesus Christ!

Appropriately, the community which the former beggar joined immediately was the worshiping community. Previously he had been forbidden to enter the area beyond the Court of the Women in the Temple. He had been denied access to God, deprived of the status of human. Jubilantly, the man pranced and danced, shouted and sang. At last, he could carry out the prayers and offerings which he had assumed he never would. Because of the Name of Jesus Christ declared through strong men who roused him from helplessness, the one-time cripple worshiped!

Perhaps you, too, have been on the sidelines of life. You may be conscious only of your limitations and weaknesses. Maybe you have done little because you have attempted little. Your physical pains and/or emotional hurts have made you relatively inactive. You have never reached your potential, you sense. With some regret, you may consider yourself a spectator rather than a participant. The chilling fog of loneliness often seems to wrap itself around you so that you feel that others see you merely as a blur in life's mist.

Possibly, you also are a kind of beggar, subsisting on crumbs of kindness which fall all too infrequently from others. You may sometimes wonder how you can keep going. Trying to survive on others' handouts of love, you sense, leads to slow starvation of the spirit. Meanwhile, you know what a grim, hungry existence daily life is, and you try to scrounge any hint or word to sustain you for one more day.

You as a type of helpless beggar may intuitively wonder if your estrangement from others may not have something to do with your estrangement from God. You and He, you subjectively understand, were meant to be close. Somehow, however, you have apparently drifted apart. Like old classmates who gradually and unintentionally stopped writing or eventually lost contact, you surmise that something has happened to the relationship. Maybe you have occasionally been at the door of a church, like the paralytic haunting the area and the crowd in God's area. You have perhaps found it empty of meaning, a worthless effort, somewhat like the class reunion with strangers you once called friends from whom you have drifted over the years. God, even in church, may still be a stranger for you.

You have been told that the *Rx* for happiness is to own a boat, get a cottage, take a cruise, treat yourself. Buy contentment. Acquire. Restless and disaffected in life? More silver and gold will solve everything, you tell yourself. After all, this is what the hours of commercials washing over your conscious and subconscious nearly every waking hour have conditioned you to tell yourself.

But our problem is not money. We may wish—even pray— for more income, more security, more comfort, more gadgets. Additional dollars, however, will not solve our real problem. God says *no* to our pleas for more silver and gold because He knows our needs are deeper.

The gospel, the power of the Strong Name, is God's gracious answer to all our prayers. The strengthening nearness of the Risen Lord brings us the healing which we need.

It is important to note that the crippled beggar apparently never saw or heard or touched Jesus. In the account in Acts, his only contact with Jesus Christ was through Peter and John, Jesus' disciples. Although Jesus was no longer physically present, the paralyzed man learned that Jesus was still ministering. The helpless invalid was astonished to discover that Jesus Christ, ministering through His followers, empowered him to stand up and walk!

Therefore, we do not need to sigh, "If only Jesus were here now!" or lament, "If I had only lived when He was here!" We do not have to fantasize what it would be like if He could help. We need not brood, "If I could somehow see Him—I could believe."

He is here! He is alive! He still imparts His awesome strength! Every time that we, His people, take seriously His communication of Self to us through Scripture and sacrament, we discover that He presents Himself by Name! By the Spirit, through the pages of Bible, and through shared loaf and cup, God pronounces His Name afresh to us. When we appropriate that Name to ourselves, His people, we realize a new identity. We carry the family name *Christians*, and stand strong in its meaning.

Western correspondents visiting Peking have discovered that in spite of severe persecution and hardship there are still Christians in Red China. One Protestant congregation, the Rice Market Street Church, still functions in Peking. During the turmoil and readjustment of the cultural revolution since 1949, the Rice Market Street Church has had to abandon most of the practices and customs usually associated with a church. Weddings, even funerals, became a thing of the past. Everything about the life of the Rice Market Street congregation had to be stripped down to the barest essentials. And what is the irreducible minimum? Significantly, the program of the Peking Protestants revolves around a weekly celebration of the Lord's Supper and weekly readings and study of lessons from the Old and New Testaments.

Perhaps the Chinese Christians may teach us something about basics. Through the fires of revolution and hostility, these believers have learned that the Name is pronounced whenever they commune together and listen together.

In our congregations, He promises to reintroduce Himself by Name when we work seriously together with Bible and covenant together at His table. He asserts that He will mobilize us to jump and dance joyously, to sing and shout gleefully. He announces that He empowers us to move into circulation in His world.

Our great strength derives from His great strength. We have absolutely no other power except the power of the Name.

13

Paul,
who begged for healing

The pain was so intense that it felt as if a huge stake had been pounded through his body from his groin to his head. It kept recurring. In his misery, he sometimes thought of the stake used to execute criminals. Paul knew the hideous details of impalement: the sharpened stake rammed up through the victim's abdominal and chest cavity until the end of the stake protruded through one of the apertures in the skull, so that the writhing dying man was skewered like an animal on a spit.

When Paul referred to his "stake," he had in mind the excruciating agony of the deadly, sharpened pole being driven through his head, impaling him with pain and helplessness.

Some translations of the Bible into English have laundered and perfumed Paul's Greek vocabulary. When these translations render Paul's description of his recurring painful ailment as merely "a thorn in the flesh" (although the Greek word means both *thorn* and *stake*), they lose some of the vivid sense of extreme suffering suggested by the term *stake.*

Thorn or stake, the suffering and weakness was acute. It first felled Paul when he, Barnabas, and young John Mark crossed from Cyprus to Pamphylia on the southern shore of Asia Minor. They intended to preach and start congregations in the area and work their way back to their home base, Antioch.

Hemmed in by the 5,000 to 9,000 foot high wall of the Taurus mountain ridge, Pamphylia is completely shielded from the cooling north winds. Steamy, low-lying coastal plains and swamps, trapping the Mediterranean sun without its bracing breezes, make the climate hopelessly humid and enervating. Predictably, Pamphylia has always been known as a deadly malarial area.

Before the germ theory of disease, malaria was thought to be caused by swamp vapors. In fact, the word malaria comes from the Italian *mala aria,* meaning "bad air." Until late nineteenth century medical research proved that malaria is caused by many species of microscopic-size parasites transmitted by the anopheles mosquito, malaria was believed to come from foul atmosphere. Long before modern science, however, malaria was feared as one of the many deadly and debilitating fevers which ravaged the world.

Humans have little natural immunity to malarial parasites. Malaria has been more common than any other major infection. Malaria has also been the number one killer through history. As recently as 1955, malaria caused 250 million cases of illness, and 2.5 million deaths. World Health Organization campaigns, using DDT sprays, have reduced the number of malaria victims in recent years. However, with the recently discovered awareness of DDT's harmful effects on the ecology, pressures are developing to curtail the use of the deterrent, and malarial deaths may increase again.

In Paul's day, there were no antidotes for malaria, no medication. The fever mounted. The ache in his head intensified.

People who have suffered from malaria have described the paroxysms of pain inside the skull in unforgettable terms. "A red-hot bar thrust through the forehead," says one. "The grinding, boring pain in the temple like the dentist's drill; the phantom wedge driven between the jaws," remembers another. "A stake," recalls Paul, with a wave of nausea.

And the temperatures! Accompanying the severe headaches are fevers which produce delirium. After the hours and hours of burning and sweating come the chills in which the victim cannot get warm enough.

Paul huddled weakly in an enormous mound of blankets after his initial attack of fever had passed. Although the hot, moist climate made most people wear as little as possible, Paul shivered and called for more covers. His teeth chattered, his body shook, and he longed to feel some sensation of warmth inside his wracked body.

The uncontrollable shaking of a malarial patient appears ludicrous to those who don't understand the effects of malaria. Malaria victims, realizing the jokes and laughter toward their "shakes," feel humiliated. Even Sir Walter Raleigh, condemned to die on the gallows, begged his jailers to arrange his execution at a particular time in the day when he was comparatively free from his malarial shaking, which he felt might be interpreted as a sign of fear.

Paul was also sensitive to his bouts of shaking and weakness. He silently accepted the caustic comments of others.

His only hope, he knew, was to get out of the fever zone. He discussed moving to a cooler area with Barnabas, his missionary-companion. Paul and Barnabas agreed that they must leave as soon as possible, and planned to head into the uplands. When Barnabas's nephew, young John Mark, decided he had had enough missionary travel and announced he was returning home, Paul was hurt and resentful. He suspected that Mark was embarrassed and annoyed with the unpredictable symptoms of Paul's illness. Besides, he needed the boy's help more than ever. Paul felt that Mark was deserting him when the going was getting toughest.

Although almost consumed with fever and exhausted by the chills, feisty Paul forced himself to travel. The route Paul and Barnabas traveled took them through rugged mountain terrain, across surging rivers, along dizzying precipices, through brigand-ridden countryside. Few can appreciate the physical and emotional drain of such a trip even for a healthy person.

Paul, half dead with fatigue and fever, stumbled behind Barnabas into the bleak hinterland of interior Asia Minor called Galatia. He knew that the people in Asia Minor thought that fever victims were being punished by God. Paul had heard too many times that fevers were sent as divine vengeance. He wondered how the townsfolk in the cities of Galatia would receive him. An ancient curse in Asia Minor ran, "May he suffer fevers, chills, torments, pallors, sweatings, heats by day and by night." Paul knew he suffered all of these humiliating and debilitating symptoms, and worried that the Galatians would think him cursed. Furthermore, he realized what a nuisance a semi-invalid was, expecially one who landed in town as a stranger.

To his relief, Paul discovered that there were people in Galatia who welcomed his and Barnabas's preaching and who didn't apparently mind Paul's physical condition or appearance. In a letter to the cluster of churches in Galatia, Paul wrote appreciatively of their hospitality. "You know it was because of a bodily ailment that I preached the gospel to you at first; [he reminded them] and though my condition was a trial to you, you did not scorn or despise me . . ." (Galatians 4:13, 14).

Unlike most other diseases which attack once and then retreat, malaria keeps recurring. Paul discovered that the episode with his "stake" was not a single isolated trial. Rather, he found himself pounded and pummeled in a never-ending series of bouts with malaria. When Paul allowed himself the luxury of a brief autobiographical reference in part of his correspondence with the church at Corinth he described the ongoing cycle of fevers and chills in the present tense, meaning specifically that he suffered continually from intermittent attacks.

To Paul, his illness began to be an overpowering obstacle to his work. Time after time, just as his work got to a crucial point, he would be struck down unexpectedly with a blinding headache, burning fever, and enervating perspiring. Even Paul's immense willpower was not enough. To his intense disgust and anger, he was reduced to half-delirious helplessness, moaning and useless, as the attack ran its course. Indeed, Paul found that his illness hindered his work with such superhuman power that he dubbed it "a messenger of Satan" (2 Corinthians 12:7). To Paul, each attack of fever struck so frequently—so crushingly— that it seemed to have the overwhelming force of the Enemy. Each new onslaught proved to be impossible to struggle against, and Paul collapsed again and again. Such waves of pain driving him repeatedly to the outer limits of human suffering, Paul was convinced, could only come from a satanic force stronger than himself.

Ever since his Damascus Road encounter with the Risen Lord, however, Paul had also been convinced that there was another force stronger than himself. In fact, Paul firmly believed that the power of God was greater than any other, including Evil. Therefore, he prayed.

He implored the Lord to intercede. Incapacitated by the waves of pain and fever which forced him to give up his evangelizing, Paul pleaded with the living Christ for healing.

None came. Drained of strength after the searing temperatures and the exhausting chills over many days, Paul impatiently waited for his body to recoup its lost vitality. He lay in his darkened sickroom, and wondered why his plea to Christ had not been answered.

Several weeks later, Paul shakily resumed his efforts for the Lord. The recent attack had seemed longer than any earlier. Paul hoped that it would be his last.

With infuriating regularity, and at times when he could least afford to take time off for illness, the telltale symptoms would appear. In the middle of the night or in the afternoon siesta, Paul would awake with his temples splitting with pain and his clothing soaking with perspiration. On two other occasions, he beseeched the Lord for relief.

In his prayers, Paul reminded the Lord that the fever was not only crippling Paul but also impeding the Lord's work. Did the Lord not realize how humiliating the disease was? The Lord did not seem to understand that the fever aroused contempt and disgust by others.

After the second bout of praying for relief, Paul asked himself if he had prayed long enough or hard enough. It seemed to Paul that his faith was as weak as his body. The thought depressed him.

The third time he prayed for relief during a seige of malaria, Paul poured it on. After all, he told the Lord, he was laboring for Him. Wasn't it obvious that Paul could do a better job of spreading the gospel if he were healed? He begged the Lord a third time to remove the stake from him.

Surely that third mighty prayer would turn the tide. The Lord would certainly answer his prayer the third time. Paul

would be healed of his stake and rise to great heights as a
teacher, writer, and theologian. His best sellers would be called
The Power of Positive Praying and *How Prayer Made Me a
Healthy Human and A Million Converts*. He could lecture
widely on how the Lord changed him from invalid to apostle in
three easy steps.

Although Paul prayed imploringly to the Lord on three separate times to have his stake removed, the story did not turn out
the way Paul had hoped. God's answer was not what Paul
wanted.

Sometimes, we find ourselves in desperate straits and turn to
a bargaining kind of praying where we state, "Look, Lord, I
deserve to have You fix things up and make it a little easier for
me. After all, I'm trying to lead a good life."

And sometimes, in spite of the convincing reasons we present, God does not answer our requests the way we demand.

Paul heard God's *no!* three times as a reply to his plea for
respite from the long, crippling malaria attacks. Finally, Paul
also heard more.

"Three times I besought the Lord about this, that it should
leave me;" Paul confesses in an autobiographical section, "but
he said to me, 'My grace is sufficient for you, for my power is
made perfect in weakness.' I will all the more gladly boast of my
weaknesses, that the power of Christ may rest upon me." The
toughened old veteran of praying and suffering adds, "For the
sake of Christ, then, I am content with weaknesses, insults,
hardships, persecutions, and calamities; for when I am weak,
then I am strong" (2 Corinthians 12:8–10).

" . . . when I am weak, then I am strong." What kind of a
paradox is this?

Paul learned to use his illness as a means of learning that the
Lord's strength was powerful enough to see him through every
difficulty. Christ provided enough help for Paul to bear every
pain and strain. In the midst of malaria attacks, Paul discovered
that, leaning more heavily on the Lord than before, he found
Christ sufficient for everything.

Paul came out of the furnace of his fevers ready to face life
or death because Jesus Christ was the center of his life.

". . . Christ will be honored in my body, whether by life or by death" (Philippians 1:20), he confidently asserted.

William Booth, the Paul-like apostle to the forgotten millions in nineteenth-century English slums, underwent a serious eye operation in the midst of his busy, useful ministry. Doctors had Booth's son, Bramwell, tell the doughty founder of the Salvation Army that he would probably be blind the rest of his life. When he heard the news, General Booth calmly answered, "I have done what I could for God and the people with my eyes. Now I shall do for God and the people what I can without my eyes."

That was the kind of robust faith Paul had! Lacking strength of his own, he learned the extent of Christ's strength. And Paul knew that he became far stronger than if God had answered his pleas and removed the stake. God's power was made perfect in Paul's weakness.

We all have our thorns or stakes at some time or another. Being human, we will protest. We may pray. Our conversations with the Lord may take on a note of whining and pleading— or even a refreshingly candid note of honesty.

St. Teresa, whose prayers were a peppery, frank dialogue with God, wrote in her journal, "Lord, when wilt Thou cease to strew our path with obstacles? And the Lord spoke to her in answer, 'Murmur not, for it is thus that I treat my friends.' At which Teresa sighed and said, 'Ah, dear Lord, and that is why Thou hast so few.' "

In our honesty with the Lord who is honest with us, we may pray begging Him to remove our stake or thorn. We may pray repeatedly, just as Paul did.

For some, God may see fit to answer our prayers by removing the thorn or stake. If he does, rejoice and give praise!

For others of us, God apparently will not see fit to take it away. If He does not, rejoice and give praise, for God still assures us, "My grace is sufficient for you" (2 Corinthians 12:9).

Robert Louis Stevenson, cursed with such frail health that he had to leave his beloved home to survive and ration his strength to a few hours of writing each day, was one who grasped the fact that God sometimes says *no* to our nagging pleas. Stevenson also understood that God's grace suffices. Stevenson even wrote an essay called, "On the Enjoyment of Unpleasant Places."

Paul, who knew a lot about unpleasant places, would have liked that title! Any man who can write, "For the sake of Christ, then, I am content with weaknesses, insults, hardships, persecutions, and calamities" (2 Corinthians 12:10), knows that even these kinds of unpleasant places can be enjoyed for the glory of God! The Lord's grace is sufficient for any place—including sickrooms.

There is an old sea tale of a sole survivor of a shipwreck who was cast up on an uninhabited island. After anxiously praying to God for deliverance, he painstakingly collected whatever he could salvage from the wreck. With pieces of the wreckage, he constructed a crude hut, and stored the few bits of valuables he had saved. Each day, he scanned the horizon for sign of a passing vessel which he could hail. God seemed to have abandoned him, however, for he sighted nothing.

One day, when he returned from a search for food, he discovered that his hut was in flames. Everything was destroyed. The worst had happened, and his situation was hopeless. Angrily, the seaman cursed God. The next day, however, a ship arrived. "We saw your smoke signal," the rescuing skipper told the shipwrecked man.

The all-powerful Lord turns even the causes of our curses into good. Paul learned this about his malaria. He discovered how foolishly inclined he was to overestimate his own revelations, his own importance, and his own plans. Through his cycle of pain and disappointment, Paul discovered also how vain, weak, and finite he was. Most of all, however, he learned to "use" his impalement of malaria to understand that Christ's goodness matches every need.

Paul learned to live with repeated onslaughts of deadly malaria, knowing that he could honor Jesus Christ even with a feverish, pain-racked body in a sweat-soaked bed. Paul accepted his stake or hedge of thorns which hemmed him in. "I can do all things in him who strengthens me" (Philippians 4:13), he explained.

Likewise, you in your impalement of pain or disappointment

of other unchangeable circumstances may praise God through your tears and temperatures. You, too, are assured by the Living Lord, "My grace is sufficient for you, for my power is made perfect in weakness" (2 Corinthians 12:9).

14

Paul, Silas, and Timothy,
who intended to do great things

No one traveled for pleasure in those days—especially through the distant reaches of Asia Minor. Missionaries Paul and Silas knew when they started their trip that it would be exhausting. However, they had work to do for the Lord, and they felt confident that He would bolster them.

Walking every mile, they first had to climb the steep ten-thousand-foot pass through the gorge known as the Cilician Gates—the main entrance from the southern coast into the high plateau of what is now Central Turkey. Paul and Silas knew the risks. Hordes of cutthroats frequently swooped down on travelers on the deserted heights. The narrow trail often clung to precipices, and a careless step sent the hapless traveler plunging to his death on the rocks hundreds of feet below. Icy mountain rivers had to be crossed and often swept victims through the rushing waters and over the falls to inevitable drowning.

The dauntless missionaries hurried through the area known as Galatia, reassuring the shaky Christians whom Paul had organized into tiny congregations on his earlier missionary trip. The new Christians in these cities had been unsettled by those inside the church who insisted that Christians had to keep the minutiae of the Jewish law. Paul and Silas repeatedly emphasized that trust in God's acceptance through Jesus Christ, not reliance on human efforts to prove one's worthiness, brought wholeness or salvation. Paul and Silas would have liked to have stayed longer with each little cluster of believers in each city.

As always, the agenda was too full, however, and they had to keep moving. The two paused long enough in the town of Lystra to convince young Timothy, whom Paul had previously introduced to the faith, to join them. The Holy Spirit seems to have set priorities on the trio's activities. Although they could have spent months in Galatia, they felt impelled to move on to organize new churches. With excellent intentions and a sure sense of strategy, Paul moved his little party out of the great West Highway. Their plans: to break fresh ground for the Lord in the greatest province of all—Asia. This senatorial province held the distinction of being Rome's wealthiest province. The Roman orator Cicero claimed, "In the richness of its soil, in the variety of its products, in the extent of its pastures, and in the number of its exports, it surpasses all other lands" *(De Imperio Gnaei Pompei 14)*. Minerals and timber abounded. The province's wealth encouraged a high cultural level. Greek was spoken everywhere. Large, free cities and temple states straddled Asia's rich alluvial valleys.

Paul shrewdly eyed those great population centers. He knew that once the gospel was planted in those cities, the Good News would fan out to the satellite towns and villages. Paul and his companions planned to evangelize the string of big cities along the valleys of the Lycus and the Maeander and the Great Trade Route. Asia, with metropolitan areas such as the great commercial and communictions center of Ephesus, the illustrious ancient capital of Pergamum, bustling Apamea, great Colossae, sophisticated Laodicea, booming Hierapolis, busy Tralles, wealthy Magnesia, proud Sardis, seaport Smyrna, big Philadelphia, industrious Lampsacus and humming Cyzicus would provide a great power base for the expansion of the church. Each of these cities, once a congregation began to flourish, would serve as a strategic location for Christ's ministry in Rome's richest province.

Paul also realized that he and his cohorts would be working in a Greek-speaking area. The three agreed that their efforts would show speedier results in these cities than in the remote, dusty provincial towns of Galatia where local dialects and native languages such as Phrygian often made communications difficult.

The three missionaries were spurred also by an awareness of the religious situation in the province of Asia. Asia, they knew, was the center for the Great Mother cult, a collection of superstitions and fertility fads linking nearly all the Greek and Roman gods and goddesses, and a hotbed of Emperor worship. The entire area was ripe for the Good News. Paul, Silas, and Timothy strained eagerly to start their activities in Asia. Each night, after a hard day's walking, they discussed their plans. In spite of their weariness, they prayed. The three missionaries expected a long and successful church-organizing itineration in Asia.

Abruptly, they cancelled their plans. Or, more precisely, the Holy Spirit cancelled their plans. Why? Asia was a key area. Why would Paul, Silas, and Timothy find themselves "forbidden by the Holy Spirit to speak the word in Asia" (Acts 16:6)?

No reasons are given in the Bible. Some scholars have suggested that the sultry climate of some of the river valleys, a hotbed of malaria, might have proved perilous to Paul, who had been so feverish and ill in such an area (Pamphylia) on his previous journey.

All we can be certain of is that the party of missionaries encountered a roadblock. God seemed to make them change their course.

Disappointed over not getting into the province of Asia, the trio of missionaries wandered north. They discussed alternate plans. The area in which they found themselves was sparsely populated. They felt like bemoaning the fact that they had been prevented from preaching in the big Greek-speaking cities of Asia.

Weary and footsore, they tried to decide on a new field for their operations. The second-best? Bithynia, of course.

Bithynia lay directly to the north, just over the next range. A great province which swept from the Bosphorus along the southern shore of the Black Sea, Bithynia pulsated with busy, bulging cities. Furthermore, these urban centers—Nicomedia, Nicea, Chalcedon and Heraclea Pontica—were Greek-speaking. Like Asia, Bithynia boasted of some of the lushest agricultural areas of the Roman Empire. Bithynia, later the favorite province of the Emperor Hadrian, was also renowned for its numerous medicinal springs.

Bithynia seemed to offer a fertile field for evangelism, and Paul, Silas, and Timothy convinced themselves that they would find the area promising. They reminded themselves of the advantages of working in a Greek-speaking population. And were there not several cities in which to organize congregations? Furthermore, those medicinal springs would prove beneficial to Paul.

To their surprise, these three churchmen found themselves thwarted a second time. Their plans to preach, teach, and plant churches were scuttled again. What kept Paul, Silas, and Timothy from going to Bithynia?

The three men wondered. The only explanation in the Acts is the plain statement, "They attempted to go into Bithynia, but the Spirit of Jesus did not allow them" (Acts 16:7).

Sometimes, when God apparently answers negatively to our plans, it is because "the Spirit of Jesus did not allow them." Through the Holy Spirit, Jesus works today. He is not a departed hero—not a deceased leader—but the Living Lord. He makes known His intentions to His community when they recognize His Lordship and seek His guidance. We are not left leaderless to fend for ourselves. The Spirit of Jesus—the Holy Spirit—continually reintroduces the One who walked in Galilee and Judea in the first century to latter-day followers in Bithynia, Boston, Bombay, Buenos Aires or Boondockville.

Sometimes, too, we discover God's *no* in life when we reflect on whether our goals are worthy of "the Spirit of Jesus." We who take seriously Jesus' leadership know that we must examine everything in the light of His life and death and Resurrection.

Those plans you have: Are the goals worthy of a Christian? Perhaps they are good goals but are they the worthiest you can set? If not, they are not in "the Spirit of Jesus." Are your means for reaching those goals in keeping with Jesus?

When we line out our aims and ambitions, we measure them

by the Spirit of Jesus. If they are in any way inconsistent with His Spirit, we will find frustration and failure. God ultimately halts that which is out of keeping with the Spirit of Jesus.

Paul, Silas, and Timothy discovered that their plans to enter Bithynia were not consonant with Jesus' Spirit. Precisely how and why, we do not know. In any event, they had to accept God's *No* Number Two.

Bewildered and discouraged, they plodded west on another long detour to nowhere. They finally walked into the coastal city of Troas.

They frankly admitted to each other that they were stalled. They had nothing to show for their efforts except tired feet and empty purses. Although they had been away for months and had covered hundreds of miles, they had accomplished zero. No sermons, no new followers, no new congregations. Their energies had been wasted on a series of wild-goose chases over the rugged terrain of Asia Minor. After zigzagging all over the map for months, they had experienced setbacks, not successes. Hadn't they tried to busy themselves with God's work? God, however, apparently had allowed them to get stuck.

Have you ever felt stuck in life? Have you ever thought that all the doors had been closed and locked behind you, and you had no future? Have you ever wondered what direction your life should take? Have you ever told yourself that roadblocks in your way kept you from doing what you would like? Perhaps you feel this way because of your job. Perhaps you think this because of the way school is going. Perhaps you are recently retired. Perhaps you are recently widowed.

Sometimes, even the church seems stalled and roadblocked. According to the *New York Times* (April 15, 1973), most mainline denominations have been experiencing net losses in membership each year for the past five years (2 to 5 percent loss for the Lutherans, Methodists, Episcopalians and Presbyterians during 1972). Giving to national church headquarters has declined. It becomes harder to make a dent in industrialized society. Overseas, there are no longer what used to be referred to as "mission fields," but nations facing the same problems of technology, ecology, in the midst of urban sprawl. Korea, for example, has half of its population now living in cities. The old day of easy success stories has passed. Missionary personnel, already severely reduced by budget crunches, face hostile governments in many areas of Africa and Asia. Although 35 percent of the world's population was Christian in 1900, it presently numbers only 30 percent. And by the year 2000, it is estimated that only 20 percent of all those on this planet will be Christian. Studying all the statistics in American churches recently lead many to conclude that the church—like many other institutions and individuals—has had most of the doors slammed for good.

Paul, Silas, and Timothy sat at Troas, conscious primarily that God had vetoed all their plans to evangelize first Asia, then Bithynia. As they looked around them, they thought of others who had passed through Troy as winners and successes. They recalled how Alexander the Great had crossed from Macedonia to Troy, rekindled his zeal at the tomb of Achilles, then set off to overthrow all the old dynasties and conquer the East. Paul, Silas, and Timothy were only four miles from the Plain of Troy, where Europe and Asia encountered each other in the epic battle described in Homer's immortal song. The Christian mission-men rested near where the mighty Xerxes reviewed his 3 million strong invasion force by which he intended to bring Europe under his sway. Reminders of such conquerors made Paul's party feel more frustrated.

At the time when the outlook seems most bleak and pessimistic, God frequently opens new doors. Sometimes, God seemingly allows roadblocks because He had bigger plans in mind for us. The apparently senseless detours and times when we seem stalled are often God's way of preparing and presenting new opportunities.

Paul, Silas, and Timothy, slumped wearily in Troas after months of cancelled plans and wasted trips, discovered that "the Spirit of Jesus did not allow them" to fulfill their dreams of church work in Asia or Bithynia because he had more important work for them across the Aegean.

Paul, Silas, and Timothy had noticed the throngs of foreign visitors in Troas. Merchants, businessmen, and seamen from European cities were a frequent sight in Troas's busy wharves, warehouses, shops, and streets. The unusual garb of Westerners always caught the eye of newcomers to Troas. Particularly noticeable was the attire of the Macedonians. Paul, Silas, and Timothy had never seen anything quite like the Greek poncho-like mantles and broad hats which acted as a combination sun shield and battle helmet worn by the Macedonians.

To their surprise one night, a man from Macedonia came to Paul and pleaded, "Come over to Macedonia and help us" (Acts 16:9). Macedonia was the last place Paul's group ever thought of visiting. Macedonia, however, happened to be top on God's priority list.

The figure of "the man of Macedonia" represented Europe. The man of Macedonia was God's agent to cry for the Good News of Jesus Christ to be brought to the Western World.

Until that time, the gospel had been confined to the Middle East. The infant church had crawled out of its Judean cradle, but had not ventured out of its front yard. When Paul's party sailed from Troas to Macedonia, the church strode into the wider Roman world and across to Europe.

Sometimes apparently insignificant, undramatic events serve as the hinge of history. Probably no one who watched three bedraggled Christian missionaries walk down the gangplank in Macedonia realized what a momentous hour it was in the history of the West. In the voyage of Paul, Silas, and Timothy to Europe, the church of Jesus Christ was carried from Asia Minor and planted firmly and permanently in Europe. Think how subsequent history of the Western world—indeed, of the entire globe—was affected!

Reversing the exact course of the Macedonian conqueror, Alexander the Great, who traveled from Europe to Troas, the Galilean Conqueror was carried from Troas to Europe. Alexander temporarily overwhelmed his adversaries, died, and left nothing except memories of a brief empire and a few inscriptions. Jesus, still welcomed as loving Lord, continues to rule. Transcending all nations and localities, the Conquering Christ makes a claim and receives acclaim from persons in Macedonia and Troas, Europe, and Asia!

At one time, the motto of the Spanish royal coat of arms

carried the Latin inscription *Ne plus ultra*—"There is no more beyond here." The Spaniards thought that they were perched on the farthest point of the world, beyond which there was nothing. When Columbus returned from his momentous voyage, the Spanish king and queen learned that there was more beyond. Their coat-of-arms motto suddenly seemed inappropriate. It was immediately amended simply by dropping the first word *Ne*. The inscription then read, *Plus ultra* ("There is more beyond").

For many, including that cluster of Christians at Troas who had received God's turndown twice, their motto might have been *Ne plus ultra*—"There is no more beyond here"—if they had reckoned without the Living Lord.

"There is no more beyond here" seemed to have been the final word for everything at Calvary. Everyone thought that Jesus was stuck—for good—on the Cross; God apparently was stalled. The dead end to beat all dead ends took place on that Hill of the Skull. *Ne plus ultra*. Nothing more.

God, however, is never helpless. He brought back Jesus from the dead. Christ's return to life assures us that God still remains in control of everything—even death. He is never stalled. He is never stuck. No roadblock can stop Him. Not even a crucifixion.

Our dismal wailing that there is no future, that God cannot cope with our crises, now proves to be totally unnecessary. *Plus ultra!* "There is more beyond!" God opens new doors. God surprises us with unexpected Macedonian invitations.

Matthew Fontaine Maury was a robust young seaman with prospects of a brilliant career as a naval officer. When he was thirty-three, he was crippled in an accident when the vehicle in which he was riding overturned. Maury, who had given his seat to a lady, was the only person injured. He was bitterly disappointed when he learned that he could never return to sea. To his intense disgust, Matthew Maury was consigned to a desk job. He was condemned to remain on land the rest of his life, but from his desk Maury worked out the principles of navigation without which no ship now sails the seas.

With God, *plus ultra.*

Carmelite Janvier, nine-year-old daughter of a socially prominent New Orleans family, was playing on the deck of the family's yacht when a miniature cannon accidentally went off. The
blast destroyed the little girl's one eye and nearly blinded the
other. It also left Carmelite Janvier tragically disfigured.

Because of her handicap, Carmelite Janvier became empa-
thetic to other children who had suffered. Eventually, she organized New Orleans "visiting teachers"—a dedicated group of
gifted educators who worked with handicapped and troubled
pupils. Carmelite Janvier pioneered in talking with hurting and
handicapped children, testing the backward, visiting broken
homes, instituting corrective speech and hearing programs. At
her urging, one of the earliest Division of Special Services was
set up in a public school system, giving particular attention to
stutterers, deaf, blind, bedridden, retarded, truant, and chronic
delinquent youngsters.

When the doors apparently crash shut, God always opens
another! When we think we are stalled, God has bigger plans
in mind.

God's bigger plans are often disclosed through "a man from
Macedonia"—the cry for help from someone in need. Paul,
Silas, and Timothy discovered that God had said *no* to their
plans to preach in Asia and Bithynia but opened the door to
preach in Europe through the plea of the man from Macedonia.

Who was this mysterious "man from Macedonia"? Luke? Perhaps. Immediately after mentioning this unnamed visitor from
Macedonia, Luke, the author of Acts, indicates that he was
present by using the term "we." Many conclude that the sudden use of "we" in the narrative indicates that Luke not only
joined the party at that point but was the Macedonian who
urged the missionaries to cross from Troas.

Luke or not, the figure represents Europe. The man from
Macedonia symbolizes the Western world crying out for word
about Jesus.

There were lots of reasons—sound, sensible reasons—not to
listen to the man from Macedonia. It was dangerous. It was risky
because there was the possibility of failure. No one had done it
before. The missionary party knew that they would be farther

than ever from their homes.

"Come over to Macedonia and help us" the man from Macedonia implored (Acts 16:9). This human cry for help was enough. To Paul, Silas, and Timothy, it was like a vision—a call from God.

God's answers often come in human requests. God has gone on record that He stands wherever there is human need. A plea for help by a brother is actually a summons for service by the Saviour! "Come over to Macedonia and help us" can be interpreted as the voice of God.

God's guidance for Paul, Silas, and Timothy came through the human voice of a visitor from across the Hellespont. God's guidance for you or me may come through the human cry of a stranger across the world, across the city, across the street, or across your kitchen table! The "man from Macedonia" comes in all sorts of sizes and shapes. Macedonian men speak in various voices and reveal many needs.

"Macedonia" today may be war-torn South Asia; the cry may come in the form of a whimper of a hungry child in a refugee camp. Macedonia may be Japan; the plea may be spoken in the form of a dozen small congregations' request for the expertise of a Christian Education consultant, or, Macedonia may be a halfway house where parolees ask for volunteers to join them occasionally for meals and recreation to help them adjust to life outside prison walls. The Macedonian call may come from a son or daughter or from a lonely shut-in nearby. The Man from Macedonia today may be a missionary who seldom gets any mail, a runaway teen-ager hitchhiking, a tired soldier waiting forlornly in a bus station, a pregnant, unwed girl, a businessman who has just learned that he has been "merged," a young veteran trying to find a job, a weary mother of three preschoolers with the sniffles. The call to "come over to Macedonia and help" may be heard everywhere there are people.

The big question for you and me is not "Why are we apparently stalled sometimes?" but "Are we listening?" Sometimes those from the Macedonias around us can only whisper or use sign language. *Help* signals often are hard to pick up. God, however, patiently waits for us to be sensitive enough to detect those signs and signals from others.

Someone near is communicating to you: "Come over and help!" Through that other, God opens new doors for you and discloses His bigger plans for you.